CAPSTONE

CW00349777

Stay Smart

Smart Things to Know About **Brands and Branding**	JOHN MARIOTTI
Smart Things to Know About **Business**	JAMES LEIBERT
Smart Things to Know About **Business Finance**	KEN LANGDON
Smart Things to Know About **Change**	DAVID FIRTH
Smart Things to Know About **Consultancy**	PATRICK FORSYTH
Smart Things to Know About **CRM**	DAVID HARVEY
Smart Things to Know About **Culture**	DONNA DEEPROSE
Smart Things to Know About **Customers**	ROS JAY
Smart Things to Know About **Decision Making**	KEN LANGDON
Smart Things to Know About **E-Business**	MIKE CUNNINGHAM
Smart Things to Know About **E-commerce**	MIKE CUNNINGHAM
Smart Things to Know About **Growth**	TONY GRUNDY
Smart Things to Know About **Innovation and Creativity**	DENNIS SHERWOOD
Smart Things to Know About **Knowledge Management**	THOMAS KOULOPOULOS
Smart Things to Know About **Leadership**	JONATHAN YUDELOWITZ
Smart Things to Know About **Life Long-learning**	ANDREW HOLMES
Smart Things to Know About **Managing Projects**	DONNA DEEPROSE
Smart Things to Know About **Marketing**	JOHN MARIOTTI
Smart Things to Know About **Mergers & Acquisitions**	TONY GRUNDY
Smart Things to Know About **Motivation**	DONNA DEEPROSE
Smart Things to Know About **Partnerships**	JOHN MARIOTTI
Smart Things to Know About **People Management**	DAVID FIRTH
Smart Things to Know About **Scenario Planning**	TONY KIPPENBERGER
Smart Things to Know About **Six Sigma**	ANDREW BERGER
Smart Things to Know About **Strategy**	RICHARD KOCH
Smart Things to Know About **Managing Talent**	STEPHANIE OVERMAN
Smart Things to Know About **Teams**	ANNEMARIE CARRACIOLO
Smart Things to Know About **Technology Management**	ANDREW HOLMES
Smart Things to Know About **Your Career**	JOHN MIDDLETON

CAPSTONE

Smart

THINGS TO KNOW ABOUT

Mergers &
Acquisitions

TONY GRUNDY

First published 2003 by

Capstone Publishing Ltd (A John Wiley & Sons Co.)
8 Newtec Place
Magdalen Road
Oxford OX4 1RE
United Kingdom
http://www.capstoneideas.com

British Library Cataloguing in Publication Data
A CIP catalogue record for this book is available from the British Library

ISBN 1-84112-086-3

Typeset by
Forewords, 109 Oxford Road, Cowley, Oxford

Printed and bound by
T.J. International Ltd, Padstow, Cornwall

This book is printed on acid-free paper

Substantial discounts on bulk quantities of Capstone books are available to corporations, professional associations and other organizations. For details contact Capstone Publishing by telephone (+44-1865-798623), fax (+44-1865-240941), or email (info@wiley-capstone.co.uk).

Contents

What is Smart?

The *Smart* series is a new way of learning. *Smart* books will improve your understanding and performance in some of the critical areas you face to-day like *customers, strategy, change, e-commerce, brands, influencing skills, knowledge management, finance, teamworking, partnerships.*

Smart books summarize accumulated wisdom as well as providing original cutting-edge ideas and tools that will take you out of theory and into action.

The widely respected business guru Chris Argyris points out that even the most intelligent individuals can become ineffective in organizations. Why? Because we are so busy working that we fail to learn about ourselves. We stop reflecting on the changes around us. We get sucked into the patterns of behavior that have produced success for us in the past, not realizing that it may no longer be appropriate for us in the fast-approaching future.

There are three ways the Smart series helps prevent this happening to you:

- by increasing your self-awareness
- by developing your understanding, attitude and behavior
- by giving you the tools to challenge the status quo that exists in your organization.

Smart people need smart organizations. You could spend a third of your career hopping around in search of the Holy Grail, or you could begin to create your own smart organization around you today.

Finally a reminder that books don't change the world, people do. And although the *Smart* series offers you the brightest wisdom from the best practitioners and thinkers, these books throw the responsibility on you to *apply* what you're learning in your work.

Because the truly smart person knows that reading a book is the start of the process and not the end . . .

As Eric Hoffer says, "In times of change, learners inherit the world, while the learned remain beautifully equipped to deal with a world that no longer exists."

David Firth
Smartmaster

Preface

Mergers and acquisitions (M&A) are an essential topic for today's senior manager. History is littered with great acquisition disasters, such as at BT, Marconi and BMW's purchase of the Rover Group.

Besides destroying shareholder value, mismanaging acquisitions can be career limiting. To undertake M&A activity without in-depth knowledge and practical experience is almost inevitably doomed to failure. Also, it is likely to swamp your existing workload (if not well managed) and cause stress of an order which is probably unthinkable.

So it is imperative that you get smart on M&A – or even smarter – to avoid these pitfalls, otherwise the consequences might be a uniquely uncomfortable level of corporate and personal pain.

Smart Things to Know About Mergers and Acqusitions will go a long way to mitigating these risks. You will learn from distilled lessons of past acquisition and merger activity – and from those who have studied it at a theoretical and practical level.

Besides these imperatives, M&A present the ultimate management challenge – both in terms of complexity of issues and of management process. This makes the topic absolutely fascinating – especially at an intellectual level.

Based originally on MBA course material and on executive seminars on M&A, *Smart Things to Know about Mergers and Acqusitions* gives you the very best of contemporary thought on M&A practice.

Tony Grundy
December 2002
a.grundy@cranfield.ac.uk

1

Introduction – Acquisitions and Growth

Acquisition logic and growth – the acquisition culture

When someone mentions the words 'acquisitions and mergers', one can perhaps be forgiven for thinking about 'stakeholder value destruction'. For in recent years we have seen the demise of a number of major corporate disasters. Witness, for example, the write-offs of billions of pounds at BT and Marconi due to ill-thought-through acquisitions.

But corporate disasters on this scale do not mean that acquisitions and mergers are inevitably doomed. Rather they underline the need to really think through the logic of any acquisition, and the alternatives (organic

SMART QUOTES

The 1990s will go down in history as the time of the biggest merger and acquisition (M&A) wave of the century. Few, if any, corporate resource decisions can change the value of a company as quickly or dramatically as a major acquisition. Yet the change is usually for the worse. Shareholders of acquiring firms routinely lose money right on announcement of acquisitions. They rarely recover their losses. But shareholders of the target firms, who receive a substantial premium for their shares, usually gain.

M. L. Sirower, *The Synergy Trap*

development and alliances). Also more small-scale and closely related acquisitions (which are astutely managed) do frequently pay off.

This book is written for present and future acquisition champions who want to steer around the rocky waters of acquisitions – securing both business success and the success of their areas.

There are a number of reasons why you might have bought this book on acquisitions and mergers. First, you may have an acquisition in mind, and wish to be guided through the process as its champion. Second, you may simply be looking to acquisition as a route for growing your business in the future. Third, you may be just readying yourself in case an unexpected acquisition opportunity crops up. Fourth, you may be looking at potentially divesting of all or part of one of your businesses, and seek guidance on the best route forward.

In this introductory chapter we will consider:

• Acquisition strategy and business growth.

• Acquisitions and shareholder value (1) types of acquisition.

• The acquisition process.

• Routes to corporate growth: acquisitions, joint ventures and investment.

Acquisitions strategy – and business growth

Acquisitions are one of the most valuable routes to business growth. But
there may well be other routes too, including organic development and
alliances.

Some acquisitions fail primarily because of poor execution, but there
are many which fail simply because of the problems inherent in the
acquisition idea – built in from the very start.

First we explore the key routes to growth generally and then we move
onto the main reasons (good and not-so-good) for companies actually
making acquisitions. We then look at the different types of acquisitions
and examine how they can add shareholder value.

The logic of acquisitions and routes to growth

As competitive challenges intensify, the pressure to find effective routes
to growth have increased. The corporate mind-set is often of striving for
continual growth, rather than for selective growth, coupled with an
ongoing review of divestment opportunities.

A few groups view their portfolio more like a deck of cards to shuffle in
order to generate sustainable increases in shareholder value. This is a
different perspective to that of considering a business – once developed
or bought – to be something to hang onto.

> Of the various opportunities for growth which may exist, the option of acquisition is by far the riskiest, unless pursued after an extended period of close collaboration with the target company as a partner.
>
> D. Faulkner and C. Bowman, *The Essence of Competitive Strategy*

Let us look at the case of Virgin, which has skilfully timed its transactions to maximize shareholder value:

- Virgin is no longer in the pop music business, having sold out to EMI in the mid-1990s.

- Virgin entered the airline industry in the early/mid-1990s to capitalize on the complacency of other major airlines.

- Virgin sold 49% of its share in Virgin Atlantic (to Singapore Airlines) at what would seem a very timely moment.

- Virgin went into cinemas in the 1990s and sold out in 1999.

- Virgin entered financial services in 1997 and announced plans to enter the mobile telephone market in 1999. It then sold Virgin Direct to the Royal Bank of Scotland.

One lesson from the Virgin experience is that acquiring a business may be for ever, or it may be appropriate for a particular time period only. A second moral is that *divestment* is always a potential option: a particular business unit might be worth more (in either just real or just perceived terms) to a different corporate parent.

So why do acquisitions generate such interest and attention anyway? Good reasons for making acquisitions might include:

(a) To gain genuine and tangible economies of scale that will manifest themselves in lower internal or bought-in costs.

(b) To get rid of corporate and business overhead which is adding little value, or which can easily be substituted by our own resource.

(c) To acquire a distinctive product or set of services which can be easily sold-on through your own distribution channels – and without significant distraction.

Notice how specific and explicit these reasons are, and also the order in which they are listed. [This is not probably the order in which you were thinking of, probably you would have listed in the order (c), (b), (a).] But the reality is that the realized value of most acquisitions is in the above order of (a), (b), (c).

Not-so-good reasons for acquiring businesses include:

- To satisfy the expectations of the stock market, which is expecting you to make a move of this kind.

- To satisfy a corporate restlessness to 'do something' – otherwise one will be going backwards.

- To acquire market share (in markets where market share may increase but will not necessarily result in gains in shareholder value).

- As a defensive measure (unless all other defensive options have been explored and exhausted – and even then if and only if it is better to stay in the business on a longer-term basis rather than to exit).

- To establish a presence in a market that is booming – but perhaps only at the moment.

- To be responding to the fact that competitors are acquiring (but aggressively they may be foolish).

- For a new management leader or team – to fulfil an agenda to be seen as having done something significant, big and bold, within the first 12–18 months.

- To fill a short- or medium-term profit gap – without ensuring first that this will provide a genuine economic profit (over and above your cost-of-capital).

- To acquire a quite new competence (unless we are really, really clear as to how you will exploit this elsewhere in the group, and what hurdles preventing effective knowledge transfer might exist).

The number of not-so-good reasons listed above for making acquisitions underlines the importance of examining why it is (precisely) you might wish to acquire businesses.

Acquisitions, alliances and organic development

The three major routes to growth are:

- Alliances

- Organic development

- Acquisitions

Each route then branches off into sub-options. Thus, alliances can lead on into acquisition, development or withdrawal (i.e. divestment). Acquisition can also lead to further organic development or selective disposal, or to restructuring. Above all, we should therefore ask the key questions:

What do we want to achieve through our strategy? What strategic options are available, and which adds most/least shareholder value?

Rather than:

Who can we do a deal with (i.e. acquire or have an alliance with)?

Research studies into how acquisitions are managed suggest that, on average, acquisitions tend to destroy rather than add to shareholder value. This fact makes it an uphill battle to generate shareholder value through acquisition, as any company that is strong and/or has lots of potential will typically be prohibitively expensive. Also, the buyer is likely to have far more imperfect information than the seller. Sadly, in general terms (except in a forced sale) divestment tends to generate far more shareholder value relative to making an acquisition.

In particular, successive management research studies unequivocally suggests that on average, acquisitions tend to destroy rather than add to shareholder value (Porter, 1987). It is invariably an uphill battle to generate shareholder value through acquisition, as any company that is strong and/or has lots of potential will typically be prohibitively expensive. (For more on shareholder value, see Rappaport, 1986; Copeland *et al.*, 1990; Stewart, 1991.)

The lesson from this is that your management team *must* consider – simultaneously – the full range of corporate development routes, and not merely acquisition.

To buy or not to buy, or to be sold

In an acquisition workshop for a medium-sized business services company, the management reviewed their options for acquisition strategy, off-site.

Using Figure 1.1, the team considered a range of options for acquiring other companies. They then turned to the option of *being* acquired (again there were several possibilities). Further, it then proved possible to achieve most of their strategic aims by a number of alliances, possibly coupled with a small acquisition. Finally, organic development through poaching an experienced team from a competitor – or simply by well-focused recruitment of an equivalent team – ended up as the most attractive option overall.

The moral of this story is that one can easily pursue the acquisition route as a default option – unless other avenues are explored more thoroughly first.

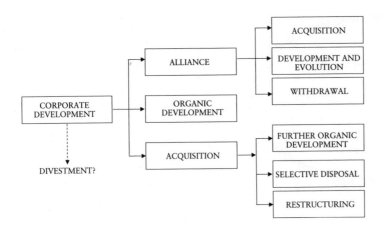

Figure 1.1 Routes to corporate development.

Below we now compare some of the perceived advantages and disadvantages of different routes to growth generally:

	Organic development	Acquisitions	Alliances and joint ventures
Advantages	Easier to control	Fast	Opens exciting opportunities
	Builds around core competencies	Extends competencies and opportunities	Transcends limited competence
	Lower risk	Surprises competitors	Surprises competitors
Disadvantages	Slower	Costly	Alliance may crumble
	May involve up-front revenue costs	Difficult and potentially risky	Collaborators may dominate
	Unlikely to surprise competitors	Hits profits
Absorbs a lot of time	Doesn't give control
Perceived lower quality earnings

But the above table does not always reflect the underlying realities, and could – at face value – be misleading for the following reasons.

First, organic development is often not perceived as being as exciting as other forms of corporate development – and slower. While it does take some time to develop a company organically, the speed with which mobile companies (like Virgin or Tesco) can move organically is impressive. Organic development may be a lot faster than managers might perceive it to be. Much can be done by accelerating organic development, for example by piloting a concept, or by assembling a team of cross-functional, internal venture managers, or by modelling what the opportunity looks like in its future market, and then working backwards to arrive at a strategy.

In some situations organic development can achieve strategic goals faster than an acquisition, which can require a lengthy integration period. Far from being fast, success can be extremely slow indeed (as our later case material on BMW's acquisition of Rover illustrates).

Acquisitions may also not lead to sustainable competitive advantage. An acquisition may temporarily throw competitors off-balance and gain temporary increases in market share, revenues and resulting profit. But if competitors then make acquisitions of their own, their beneficial effect is quickly reversed. For example, KPMG (a merger between PMM and KPMG Thomson McLintock) was once hailed as 'the biggest accounting firm in the world'. This was indeed true but only for about five minutes, until this move was leapfrogged by other members of the Big Six accounting firms.

Indeed, the very word 'merger' is often synonymous with acquisition; mergers are rarely – if ever – between equal partners and the word itself can actually mislead staff expectations and lead to disaffection and key people leaving, again destroying shareholder value.

Acquisitions that prove very difficult can not only absorb a lot of scarce senior management time (and thus destroy value), but may detract from other value-creating activities, especially:

• Organic development

• Alliances (which might sometimes achieve strategic goals more effectively and at lower cost)

• Maintaining and protecting the performance of core operations

Acquisitions appear to have an artificial handicap both in terms of having a strategic and a financial headstart.

A *strategic head-start* arises usually because acquisitions are typically seen as aggressive moves that reposition the business or group almost immediately. Acquisitions are labelled 'strategic' because they are bold but not necessarily because of their carefully thought-through logic.

Second, a *financial head-start* can arise because acquisitions may not be exposed to the same financial rigours as internal investment decisions. Managers may frequently focus on 'the multiple of current earnings' as a benchmark assessment of target company value. This is worthwhile illustrating further here – although this will be expanded on in Chapter 6 on 'Financial Evaluation'.

Because future earnings streams are viewed as being relatively unpredictable, the rigours of discounted cash flow may often be bypassed or made a subsidiary consideration. Also, the basis for assuming current earnings will be sustained (or, indeed, grown) may not be very thoroughly challenged. This challenge needs to focus on any changing competitive conditions, or potential erosion of competitive position.

Valuing a business using future earnings

For example, suppose we take an acquisition target which has current (post-tax) earnings of £30 million. Assuming that these earnings are sustainable, an earnings multiple of 12 would value the company at £360 million. But if £5 million of these earnings (after tax) are derived from a product which is unavoidably to become obsolescent, then the sustainable earnings are a mere £25 million. The value of the company is thus 12 times £25 million, or just £300 million.

To summarize, hopefully this discussion has put more caution back into your acquisition process and philosophy. While successful acquisitions do exist, it is imperative that you start off with the mind-set that the odds of generating sustainable shareholder value through acquisitions are generally against you. In order to move the odds upwards you do need to possess 'best-in-class' knowledge (which this book aims to provide) shared with the management team – and a mature, detached and commercially astute attitude.

While organic investment is frequently subjected to a tough appraisal regime, acquisitions are sometimes given an inappropriate strategic and financial head-start, which can be severely regretted when the acquisition fails to live up to its longer-term expectations.

Intensive involvement in acquisition search, deal-making and integration can also absorb a lot of scarce senior management time (and thus destroy value). It may also detract from other value-creating activities, especially:

- Alliances (which might sometimes achieve strategic goals more effectively and at lower cost)

- Maintaining and protecting the performance of core operations

- Organic development: just outside the current business scope

So let us now look first at the various types of acquisitions (each of which may give rise to differing financial rewards and risks), and also the acquisition process and critical success factors. This will help us to understand more clearly how acquisitions can generate real shareholder value.

How acquisitions can add, dilute or destroy shareholder value

Acquisitions, as has been pointed out, do not necessarily create shareholder value. But why is this the case? Acquisitions are frequently mismanaged because of the build-up of untested commitment, over-enthusiasm and the 'thrill of the chase' (Jemison and Sitkin, 1986). Anyone who has ever been involved in an acquisition should quickly recognize what we mean. It is very hard (even with the best of intentions) to maintain objectivity and complete clarity about the rationale and value of an acquisition once the process gets under way. Frequently it is the divesting company (and not the acquirer) that actually generates more value.

Understanding potential shareholder value creation is very much not simply a matter of playing around with the financial numbers. These numbers require concrete, strategic support and analysis. One useful framework to help us to think through the shareholder value of an acquisition strategy is that of the 'three V's'

- V1 is the value inherent in the business strategy itself

- V2 is the value added through the particular deal

- V3 is the value created or destroyed through post-acquisition management

The key test should therefore be: 'Why and how do you claim to be adding value through acquisition? Is it V1, V2 or V3 or some combination of these?'

Examining our three Vs (which are implicit in McTaggart *et al.*, 1994) closer, V1 can be assessed by evaluating a variety of parameters, which we expand on later.

KILLER
QUESTIONS

What is V1 for one of your targeted acquisitions?

- Are its markets growing and relatively free from competitive pressure?

- Is the acquisition's competitive position 'strong', 'average' or 'weak', not merely currently but against changing customer and competitive needs?

- Does the acquisition fit the existing competitive strategy of your own core business?

- Is its competitive position supported by underlying sources of competitive advantage? Are these sources of competitive advantage hard or easy to imitate?

The above four tests are tough and may help to weed out those whose financial health seems to be reasonable but whose strategic health is ailing.

The next 'V test' is V2: what is the value added through the particular deal? To arrive at V2 you need to assess the financial consequences of the strategy (in terms of anticipated cash flows), and also the underlying value of business assets and liabilities. To what extent are you paying more than, or less than, a reasonable value for these cash streams or assets?

McTaggart *et al.* (1994) describe the V2 as 'the bargain value' of the acquisition. Some companies (notably Hanson PLC and Hanson-lookalikes) have built corporate fortunes through exploiting V2 (and also, as will be shown later, V3). One very clear sign of V2 at work is where an acquirer buys a group for, say, £10 million, then makes disposals which yield at least £10 million, and is still left with one or more very profitable businesses.

In assessing the bargain value (or 'V2') you also need to take into account the underlying investment requirements and cost of changes necessary to sustain assumed cash flows.

V3 – the value added or destroyed during integration – is another tough test. Even where V1 and V2 are positive, V3 can be negative through ill-advised post-acquisition management.

Having explored routes to corporate development (including acquisitions), different types of acquisitions, and also how they can add value, the different management perspectives on acquisitions are now examined.

For the same acquisition which you looked at in the previous exercise, ask your-self these questions to focus on V1 and V2:

- Was the deal done at a total cost (deal price plus investment and change costs) which was particularly favourable (relative to cash flows and the underlying value of net assets), or not? (V2)

- Was post-acquisition management conducted in a way which created or destroyed value? (V3)

- Overall, did the acquisition appear to add to or destroy value? (V1 + V2 + V3)

Acquisitions and shareholder value (1) – types of acquisition

There are many ways of distinguishing between types of acquisition. These include ones which differentiate between ten variables:

- Scope: 'in-fill' versus 'step-out'

- Relatedness: 'related' versus 'diversification'

- Geographic coverage: 'local' versus 'cross-border'

- Style: 'friendly' versus 'hostile'

- Company status: 'public company' versus 'private company'

- Intention: 'deliberate' versus 'opportunistic'

- Purpose: 'defensive' or 'protective' versus 'offensive'

- Predictability of value: 'calculative' versus 'speculative'

- Strategic mode: 'development' versus 'turnaround'

In general the acquisition strategy is one that should be employed with great caution. The more closely related the business of the acquisition candidate is to the business of the acquirer, typically the less the risk there is, since the new owner will be familiar with the major problems likely to be encountered, and experienced in dealing with them. An acquisition of an unfamiliar company in an unrelated area of business from both a market and a product viewpoint is therefore the highest-risk strategy of all, and should be resisted if at all possible.

The major exception to this general rule is when the acquiring company's core competence is in company appraisal, acquisition and financial management (e.g. Hanson).

D. Faulkner and C. Bowman, *The Essence of Competitive Strategy* (1995)

• Management change: 'incremental evolution' versus 'management buy-in or bring in'

In terms of uncertainty and risk, the descriptions on the left tends to entail a lower uncertainty and risk, and the descriptions on the right, higher uncertainty and risk.

The above highlights graphically the range of possible types of acquisition: by and large each acquisition has its own almost unique blueprint – unless of course you establish up-front precisely which kinds of acquisition you are contemplating and why and stick just to those.

To give a concrete example, BMW's acquisition of Rover Group could be characterized as follows:

• Scope: step-out (four-wheel-drive and smaller cars) – high risk

• Relatedness: medium to low – high risk

• Geographic coverage: cross-border – high risk

- Style: friendly – low risk

- Company status: part of a public company – low risk

- Purpose: a mixture of defensive and offensive – medium risk

- Predictability of value: this was largely speculative – high risk

- Strategic mode: a turnaround – high risk

- Management change: initially some management, then managers brought in from BMW – high risk.

On six out of ten counts the acquisition of Rover by BMW was high risk, just two were medium risks and only two were low risk. This suggests that BMW had an immense challenge on its hands, irrespective of the particular issues peculiar to Rover Group itself.

Let us now look at these acquisitions categories in more depth.

By 'in-fill' we mean operations that are easily absorbed into existing operations, or can run along very similar lines (and without much special effort) as the other businesses. Generally speaking, these will be smaller in scale to step-out operations, which take one into new business areas (with certain exceptions).

'Relatedness' is driven by a number of factors, particularly:

- Market relatedness (and similarly of customer needs)

Smart things to remember about relatedness

- Relatedness of competencies is probably the most critical thing to align
- Success is related closely to your ability to learn

- Product and service relatedness

- Relatedness of competencies

Geographic coverage: cross-border acquisitions are generally more risky and uncertain because of a variety of cultural and regulatory factors. There is often less intimacy (of the acquirer) with local product markets and indeed with local labour markets. Add to that problems of physical distance, and sometimes even of differences in time zones, and you have a significant increase in difficulty, uncertainty and risk.

Style: friendly deals are in a different ball-game from hostile bids. A hostile bid is much more demanding in terms both of preparation and of management time. One hostile bid can easily absorb the amount of time and attention from top management of a multiple of friendly deals.

Company status: public companies tend to be better regulated externally than private companies – having perhaps (although not always) management accounts and forecasts of greater reliability than in a private company context. Stakeholders in public companies are likely to be slightly less emotional over their businesses than an owner/manager, who is likely to be more subjective about its value, and attached at a deeper emotional level.

Predictability of value: 'calculative value' occurs where it is possible to estimate – within reasonable limits of forecasting accuracy – the potential economic value of an acquisition. 'Speculative value' is where this estimation is less realistic. Examples of speculative values are put on dot-com companies in 1999 and 2000 (before the dot-com bubble burst), and also of the bids made for mobile telephone licences.

Strategic mode: while it is not always possible to discern whether a company actually is in a turnaround mode or not, warning signs could be:

- Mature product lifecycles

- Excessive cost cutting

- Complacent management

- Pending competitive entry by new sources of aggressive competition

- Under-investment over a period of years in the business

Management change: 'organizational evolution' means leaving the existing structure unchanged or making incremental changes. A management buy-in means substantial or total replacement of the existing management team, either internally or externally.

Smart ways of assessing acquisition risk

For one acquisition that you have either already made or are thinking of making, score it as follows:

	1 = low risk	2 = medium risk	3 = high risk

Scope

Relatedness

Geographic (local versu cross-border)

Style (friendly versus hostile)

Status (public versus private)

Purpose (defensive/offensive)

Predictability of value

Mode (development versus turnaround)

Management change needed

Now check your total scores, which are merely indicative:

Score: 9–13   comfortable risk

Score: 14–17   moderate risk

Score: 18–22   watch out!

Score: 23–27   potentially designed to fail

Acquisitions and shareholder value (2) – segmenting the value

Acquisitions, as has been pointed out, do not necessarily create share-holder value. This is true for a variety of reasons. Acquisitions are frequently mismanaged because of the build-up of untested commit-ment, over-enthusiasm and the 'thrill of the chase'. It is very hard (even with the best of intentions) to maintain objectivity and complete clarity about the rationale and value of an acquisition once the process gets under way. This is one of the reasons why, as we mentioned earlier, it is frequently the divesting company (and not the acquirer) that actually generates more value.

The acquisition process

The acquisition process has five main stages:

- *Strategy and objectives:* unless an acquirer is very clear about its cur-rent strategic position and intent, then the acquisition may have a spurious fit to the acquirer's goals.

- *Search:* unless very clear criteria are set for screening acquisition tar-

Dreams of synergy lead to lofty acquisition premiums. Yet virtually no attention has been paid to how these acquisition premiums affect performance. Perhaps this is because the concept of synergy itself has been poorly defined . . . the easiest way to lose the acquisition game is by failing to define synergy in terms of real, measurable improvements in competitive advantage.

A quantifiable post-merger challenge is embedded in the price of each acquisition. Using the acquisition premium, we can calculate what the required synergies must be. Often this calculation shows that the required performance improvements are far greater than what any business in a competitive industry can reasonable expect.

M.L. Sirower, *The Synergy Trap* (1997)

gets (strategic do's and don'ts), then the search process will be unfocused and misdirected.

- *Evaluation:* evaluation demands both qualitative and quantitative analysis to link the perspectives of strategy, marketing operations, organization and finance.

- *Deal-making:* although this is a crucial part of the process, it is only one of the stages when things can go right or wrong. Also, during the deal-making process the strategic assumptions coming out of the first two stages will need extensive checking out.

- *Integration (or post-acquisition management) and learning:* during this phase any changes to management, operations and to strategy are implemented and there is further development via new opportunities or harvesting synergies.

Which of these phases have your organizations frequently done (a) well or (b) not-so-well, and in the case of (b), why?

Integrating management perspectives – strategic, financial, organizational, tax, legal

Managing acquisition demands mastery of a number of quite differing perspectives. These include:

- *The strategic perspective:* understanding corporate goals, acquirer and target's strategic position, market, customer and competitor analysis.

- *The financial perspective:* understanding past performance and drivers of future performance, appreciation of financial strengths and vulnerabilities, and of net assets.

- *The organizational perspective:* understanding of organizational strengths, weaknesses and vulnerabilities, including dependencies on top management skills and other critical competencies, organizational culture and effectiveness of processes.

- *The taxation perspective:* appreciation of the likely tax consideration around potential deals and of different deal structures and their implications.

- *The legal perspective:* understanding the detailed process of negotiating the contract for sale, the role of warranties and indemnities, etc.

Managing these corporate perspectives can be demanding on the skills set of your management team.

Try this next exercise to establish how strong you are likely to be.

Evaluating the skills of your management team

	Skills level*				
	Very strong	Strong	Average	Weak	Very weak
	5	4	3	2	1
Strategic analysis					
Market knowledge					
Financial analysis					
Operational knowledge					
Organizational analysis					
Taxation					
Legal					
Negotiating skills					
Project management					

*Note: you can (quite legitimately) also rate the skills of the assumed external advisers whom you hope to employ, as a separate exercise.

The following areas need to be covered under each phase of the process. These are defined through a number of key questions, so that you can identify any key gaps in your thinking.

Scoping your acquisition work throughout the acquisition process

Strategy and objectives

- What is your own strategic position currently?

- How might an acquisition strengthen this position?

- How does an acquisition contribute to (specifically) your corporate goals and objectives?

- Does an acquisition potentially detract from or distract you away from achieving your corporate goals and objectives?

- What is the potential opportunity cost of pursuing a particular acquisition opportunity (*vis-à-vis*, for example, organic development or alliances) or of foregoing a future acquisition opportunity?

Search

- Which competitors might you acquire?

- Are there opportunities for integrating operations with distributors or customers, or with suppliers (this is sometimes called 'vertical integration')?

- Are there businesses in slightly differing product/markets which can exploit your competencies?

- Which broking intermediaries may it be useful to contact (merchant banks, etc)?

Evaluation

- What are key market trends and are these sustainable?

- What is the prognosis for the company's external competitive position?

- What are the company's key organizational strengths and weaknesses?

- What is the financial performance strength of the target?

- What do (realistic) future cash flow projections look like?

- What specific legal, employment and pension, environmental factors might impact on the specific acquisition?

- What are the key legal stumbling blocks likely to be?

- What are the key uncertainties and risks, and what is their potential impact?

Deal-making

- Who will lead your negotiations, and what is their game plan?

- Who are they up against, and what negotiating strategy might the vendors adopt?

- How will specialist legal, taxation, employment and pensions and other factors specific to this case impact on negotiations?

- Who else might the vendor sell the business to?

Integration and learning

- Who will lead the integration process (and, where appropriate, the integration team)?

- How will it be project managed?

- What is the integration strategy, and what style will it be conducted through?

- What are the key uncertainties during integration, and how will these be managed?

- What performance goals and milestones will be laid down, and how will managers be incentivized to meet them?

- How will the effectiveness of integration be renewed, and any learnings drawn out?

KILLER QUESTIONS

So you think you have got a robust acquisition process?

1. Are you very clear as a management team what your strategic goals are – and what your own current strategic position?

2. Are you doing it for the wrong reasons (e.g. the pure pursuit of growth, sheer ambition, excitement, prestige)?

3. Is the acquisition team project manager likely to show strong, clear leadership throughout the process?

4. Will the acquisition close down other options prematurely (e.g. organic development, alliances or other acquisitions)?

5. Has the team a balanced mix of skills and can (as a whole) manage all the perspectives of strategic, financial, organizational, tax and legal?

6. Is the team sufficiently experienced (in managing acquisitions) and not learning on-the-job?

7. Has the team enough spare time and capacity to devote to the process – without undermining their present jobs?

8. Is the team likely to succumb to the thrill or the pressure of the acquisition chase?

9. Is rivalry for the target (from other buyers) not so high that 'V2' (the value generated, diluted or destroyed from the deal) becomes negative?

10. In the urge to accomplish a deal have you missed 'The One Big Thing' which is not so obvious, and which could materially hamper the success of the acquisition.

SHORT
EXERCISE

These critical success factors now pave the way for our next chapter on developing an acquisition strategy.

Alternatives to acquisition – alliances

Alliances – their role

As Jack D. Sparkes put it in *Mastering Strategy*:

> The primary short-term goal of an alliance is to obtain immediate access to your partner's capabilities. . . . The primary longer-term goal is to learn as much as possible about your partner's capabilities and competitive environment. . . . A successful alliance strategy requires (careful) pre-planning, post-alliance education, and alliance management capabilities.

Like acquisitions, alliances are therefore *not* management-as-usual. They require a very specific set of skills and an adjustment to the normal management mind-set. Alliances are essentially about being entrepreneurial, collaborative – and strategic – simultaneously.

Going into the key benefits of alliances and joint ventures more deeply, these can be listed as:

• Giving access to markets which otherwise would be difficult or impossible.

- Sharing and reduction of costs (e.g. R&D, distribution).

- Pre-empting and closing down alliance opportunities that competitors would otherwise exploit.

- Enabling the company to compete against bigger players on an equitable basis.

- Developing existing competencies – or acquiring new ones.

- Alliances both open up new opportunities and enable existing constraints to be surmounted.

But a crucial test is to ask the question: Are the assumed competitive and financial benefits of the alliance both capable of being *captured* by us within the alliance – given our relative power, and are these benefits likely to be sustainable longer-term?

The costs of an alliance can include:

- The investment – in shared assets (or own assets)

- Management effort, energy and time

- Other potential alliances foregone

- Developing organically (or by acquisition) – opportunities foregone

While we have earlier assumed that alliances *minimize* investment, considerable resources are often needed to make an alliance effective (unless it is very loose and fluid). These are often underestimated by one or more of the alliance partners, resulting in disaffection.

Exploring some of the risks now, we have:

- The other alliance partner(s) emerges as dominant.

- The erosion, and ultimately loss, of own core competencies.

- Over-protection of one's competencies (or by collaborators) makes it difficult (or impossible) to generate real synergies.

- Medium-term success is achieved – but then in the longer term the alliance breaks down because of unforeseeable reasons.

- Culture clash/mismatched expectations between partners.

In conclusion, strategic alliances thus appear to be relatively high risk, both in terms of the value of their likely pay-off and its likelihood.

Alliances – their evolution

Figure 1.2 gives a dynamic overview of how alliances may develop and evolve over time. First, they might be the product of a 'deliberate' strategy (Mintzberg, 1994): that is, one which has been targeted and

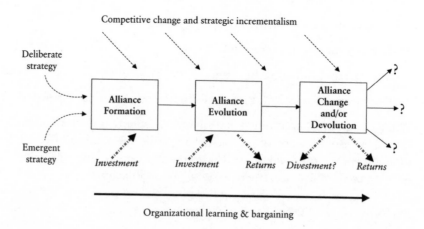

Figure 1.2 The dynamics of strategic alliances. (Adapted from Faulkner, 1995).

SMART QUOTES

thought-through against its external and internal context, longer as well
as shorter term. A deliberate strategy is one that comes from reflective,
strategic thought rather than through an opportunity merely popping-
up.

An emergent strategy is one that happens either by accident or by skilful
positioning. An opportunity arises (or is created) by a meeting or by net-
working, and this gives rise to a collaborative arrangement.

As the alliance forms there is incoming investment of time, resources
and commitment by the various alliance partners. As the alliance
becomes operational, inevitably it evolves in interaction with the market
and with competitive forces and change. New strategic decisions are
made (often incrementally, rather than as a systematic pattern), resulting
in further evolution of the alliance.

As managers move through the alliance organization (in and out) and
also within the collaborator's core organizations, there is further
change. Stakeholder management is crucial within alliances. Alliance
staff can take on their own culture and then decide to stay or to move
back to their original organizations, or to move on.

Partners to the alliance can come and go, some becoming more or less
dominant, and more or less interested in the alliance. (Honda in the

BMW–Rover case bears testimony to the impact of longer-term alliance change, with Honda becoming increasingly dominant over time over Rover.)

Ultimately, the alliance may devolve (or dissolve) – its *raison d'être* having changed or disappeared. For example, the Virgin alliance with Norwich Union in the 1990s, called Virgin Direct, lasted under two years before both partners went it alone. (Whether either or both partners anticipated this would happen from the start but pretended otherwise is an interesting open question.)

Over the alliance's lifetime there are changing patterns of investment and of returns. The financial payback of the alliance plays a profound impact over its evolution.

The critical success factors of alliances can now be quickly summarized as:

- The ability to learn from one's partners one's own deficient competencies

- The sensitivity to cultural differences and cultural fit

- The willingness to be 'transparent' to permit knowledge transfer

- Partners having complementary assets and competencies – strategic fit

- A mutual support and trust

- A strong need to collaborate exists

- Getting set-up arrangements right (including provision for divorce)

- Good and complementary management evolution – in strategy, structure, style is encouraged as the alliance develops.

Two of the areas above should now be expanded upon more fully. First, one *must* be prepared to learn from one's partners the things that one is *not* good at, otherwise one will not be able to transfer skills to other areas of operation, nor will one be left with much of one's involvement in the alliance cases.

Also, unless there is genuine sensitivity to cultural differences, then again the alliance is likely to fail. This, especially if coupled with a resistance to transfer knowledge, will frustrate the alliance to the point at which it may break up. Here, too, lies a paradox: the more open one is to sharing skills and knowledge, the more one's partners *may* open up and the alliance benefits. But, the more open one is the more of one's own competitive advantage might be leaked to a future competitor. But if one is overly mindful of the latter (competitive threat) the alliance will not work effectively, or will be severely limited.

Finally, I have included in my list the importance of set-up arrangements 'including provision for divorce'. This might sound slightly odd but as *few strategic alliances exist after five years and even fewer after ten years* some provision for divorce is essential.

Sadly, there is still limited evidence that many managers are taking fundamental questions like this seriously – until they themselves are subject to a break-up bid.

Divestment

Besides acquisitions and alliances, divestment is also an option, both for existing businesses, and also for parts of acquired businesses to which you cannot easily add economic value.

Ten lessons for the divesting owners/management

1. What features of the market environment can you emphasize as being attractive (especially the growth drivers)?

2. What past competitive strengths can you identify and extrapolate out into the future, emphasizing dominance or near dominance in key segments?

3. What is your future opportunity stream and what would it be worth as an upside if you had more funds to invest (i.e. from the acquirer)?

4. How can you create real or imagined rivalry for a deal and which new parent would it be worth most to?

5. What is the *lowest* cost of capital which could be used to discount our cash flows (and how could we justify this)?

6. What is the *highest* realistic terminal value – at the end of the forecast time horizons, and how can we justify this?

7. How can we best convey the impression that we are not in a hurry to do a deal – and we might not need to do one anyway?

8. What are the particular agendas on the acquisition team's minds (especially personal and political), and how can we exploit 'loose bricks' in the acquisition team's bid strategy?

9. What synergies with the acquirer's business value system (real or imagined) can you envisage and what 'best value' can be put on these?

10. What is the 'best case' for achieving 'sweat value' for integration and how can this be built into *our plans and forecasts* – 'we will do it anyway'?

Even where a company you have acquired or developed is profitable and has longer-term potential, four questions still need to be asked in the context of corporate development:

- How much shareholder value can be added by the centre to this business unit in future?

- How does this compare with what other corporate parents could add to the business?

- Could we sell the business to another corporate group for more than what it is worth to us (based on real or perceived market value)?

- Could we generate incremental shareholder value by reinvesting the proceeds in more exciting opportunities ourselves? (And ones that we would unlikely to be able to fund otherwise.)

The structure of the book

These five phases of acquisition – strategy and objectives, search, evaluation, deal-making and integration – form the main structure of the rest of our text (see Figure 1.3).

The key routes to corporate growth are first examined, before moving onto the main reasons (good and not-so-good) for companies actually

Figure 1.3 The acquisition process.

acquiring. The different types of acquisitions are explored before turning to how they can add shareholder value. Finally, the challenge of integrating perspectives is examined, along with the stages in the overall acquisition process and some critical success factors for getting this right. During this and other sections there are a number of short case examples, exercises, for you to complete, and (where appropriate) checklists to prompt reflection.

Summary

Acquisitions more often fail than succeed. Success can be measured in terms of shareholder value generation alongside the perceptions of other stakeholders including management, staff and customers. It is imperative therefore to consider *all* avenues to growth, including organic development, alliances and even divestment of lower potential businesses.

There are many reasons why acquisitions might be thought to be attractive. Some of these reasons are good – and some are not so good. As a potential acquirer you need to be absolutely clear on what your real reasons are, and whether these are actually appropriate. The best reasons concern the generation of sustainable increases in shareholder value. An overarching, critical success factor is to maintain an objective and dispassionate mind-set throughout the process.

There are many different types of acquisitions – and this means that each one will have its own set of issues and set of risks. Unless you are embarking on a series of acquisitions of a very similar nature, they will vary considerably in their demands placed on you during the acquisition process. Each acquisition then becomes a unique project.

Further, the value of an acquisition is made up of the inherent value of the target (V1), the value generated, diluted or destroyed during the deal (V2), or the value created or destroyed during integration (V3). V1, V2 and V3 are helpful concepts in performing a quick and dirty evaluation of an acquisition.

Acquisitions demand – perhaps more so than any other issue in management – perspectives from the strategic, financial, organizational, tax and legal viewpoints. This puts major burdens on the skill-set of your project team – including management and its advisers. Unless your team has the most important skills on board it is likely that your acquisition process will not prove effective.

2

The Acquisition Strategy

Introduction – championing the strategy

The champion of the acquisition strategy is one who is not only able to put energy into its case but one who is also strategically astute. This means being aware of your target's position, its options and its fit with your own position and with your options. To be an effective champion requires drive and commitment coupled with a rare quality in the acquisition context – objectivity.

An acquisition champion should be like a keen detective – diligent and committed, but who only charges the suspect when sufficient evidence has been collected – and also when there is 'no better suspect'.

But all too often managers acquire a company without having a particularly clear notion of what their strategy is going to be. While they at

A large number of studies have indicated that acquisition strategy often fails, and that the only people certain to gain are the shareholders in the acquired companies. The balance of evidence is that, in aggregate, acquisitions are of no net benefit to the acquiring companies. Yet businessmen continue to make acquisitions, including hostile ones, with great determination.

R. Koch, *The Financial Times Guide to Strategy* (1995)

least have some acquisition goals, the 'how' of that strategy is often left open, leaving them as unguided champions. If there is a strategy then it is essentially one an 'emergent' kind – that is, where the form of the strategy is not evident before the event but only afterwards. Here strategy is merely 'a pattern in a series of decisions and actions' (Mintzberg, 1994).

Where acquisitions are concerned it is extremely dangerous to have an open, or 'emergent' strategy. In order to capture shareholder value from an acquisition it is imperative to have a strategy that is primarily 'deliberate'. A deliberate strategy is one where: 'There is a clear, deliberate and detailed plan of achieving our goals – and with competitive advantage.'

For acquisitions, this involves having not only an idea of how your target will be developed in its external markets, but also in internally: which embraces the integration strategy too.

The crucial additional ingredient here is the idea of competitive advantage, which means that an average plan does not really count as a strategy. Put in even more everyday terms an even better definition of 'strategy' is perhaps: 'The Cunning Plan' (with apologies to Blackadder).

'The Cunning Plan'

In the Blackadder video 'Back and Forth', Blackadder and Baldrick become marooned in a time machine in the past, unable to find their way back into the present. They fail to find a way back, until Baldrick says:

'I think I have a cunning plan.'

'I am not optimistic' says Blackadder.

'You know when people die, their whole life flashes before them' – Baldrick.

'Yes? . . .' – Blackadder

'Well, if you were to stick your head into a bowl of water and waited till the very moment you were about to die then you would suddenly remember the settings (on the time machine) and we could find our way back to the present' – Baldrick.

'I have an even better idea . . .' – Blackadder, knocking him out with his fist and putting his head down the toilet.

The morale: a 'cunning' plan has surprise, is innovative, and is fundamentally simple.

Many acquisitions do not succeed because they either have an average (and not cunning) plan, or perhaps a very incomplete plan for what happens next following the acquisition.

'Competitive advantage' is also an important concept for making acquisitions. This can be defined as *either adding more perceived or real value to our customers than our competitors do, or adding a similar level of value but at lower unit cost.*

This helps us to focus our acquisition strategy more towards securing and harnessing greater customer value or towards reducing costs. These are the highly tangible products of an acquisition – and are not ancillary or incidental benefits like 'penetrating an exciting new market'.

Things that might count as a 'cunning plan' might include:

- Doing a management restructuring (as part of the integration process) at senior level to promote some thrusting, younger middle-level mangers and to incentivize them to achieve stretching, post-acquisition targets, perhaps letting go of the existing directors.

- Instead of moving in staff from the acquired company into our own premises (and they exacerbating cultural differences) to move all staff from both acquirer and target to a new, greenfield site.

- Prior to defining the new business processes and structure (in detail), to benchmark world-class organizations in order to establish best practices which will then be integrated with the best processes of both acquirer and acquired.

The final main ingredient in championing an acquisition strategy is to understand the target's market and competitive environment in more depth – especially short and medium term. Often within twelve to twenty-four months, sudden shifts in this environment can create new trading conditions – which will either help or hamper the delivery of assumed post-acquisition performance. Here environmental analysis does not always have to be 'long-range' to highlight major threats or opportunities.

KILLER
QUESTIONS

Thinking about a past, current or pending acquisition:
- Did (does) it actually have a complete strategy for the post acquisition phase?
- Did (does) this strategy actually amount to 'a cunning plan'?
- If so, what exactly was (is) cunning about it, and what value did it add?
- If not, what was (is) the value potentially destroyed by not having 'a cunning plan'?

In the remainder of this section the following areas are now examined:

- Strategy and objectives

- Evaluating options

- Determining criteria – the do's and don'ts

- Detailed evaluation – external

- Detailed evaluation – internal

- Process considerations

Strategy and objectives

Many acquisition champions feel that that they know their own strategy and position quite well, but this perception is often misplaced. Often this perception is based on some relatively basic strategy tools like SWOT (strengths and weaknesses, opportunities and threats) analysis, and upon patchy data on the market and on competitors (which is mostly backward-looking, and based on subjective impressions about the business). It is not surprising that most strategies (and this is true right up to the very large company) are partially if not substantially 'emergent' (as defined by Mintzberg, 1994).

Although many corporate parents believe that they can create value through astute corporate development decisions, the evidence suggests that they are often wrong. For example, companies frequently overpay for acquisitions.

M. Gould, A. Campbell and M. Alexander, *Corporate-level Strategy* (1994)

SMART QUOTES

Strategic goals, are also frequently defined in terms of:

(a) The extremely broad (and often vague) objectives continued in mission statements; or

(b) The highly detailed, quantitative and internal targets for financial performance contained in financial projections.

The problems with the kind of high-level goals (or rather, aspirations) in (a) above cast in stone in mission statements is that they are really too vague, timeless and open to multiple interpretations to be of much help to focus the acquisition strategy. Equally, when management are focused upon delivery of much more specific financial projections (as in b), the financial numbers often become predominant in management thinking.

These goals (for the business and for an acquisition) can usefully be structured as follows:

- *Market positioning goals:* for example, to become established and strong in markets a, b, c, etc. where there are favourable opportunity streams, and where we can exploit and grow our natural competitive advantages.

- *Competitive goals:* to exploit this market position for specific product/market/technology sectors.

- *Customer goals:* to be perceived by our customers as delivering the value of our brand promise.

- *Organizational goals:* to acquire and develop key management and technical competencies.

- *Financial goals:* to achieve specific financial targets for example in terms of:

  – turnover growth;

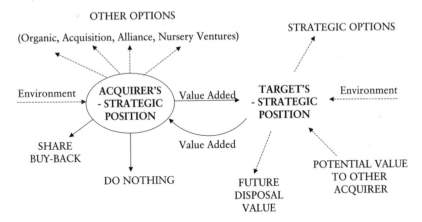

Figure 2.1 *The acquisition strategy big picture.*

- historical profit growth/growth in earnings per share;

- returns on capital employed;

- economic profit, etc.

Before acquisition options are explored, Figure 2.1 now gives us a useful framework through which we can understand the overall strategy for acquisitions. This figure emphasizes the need to understand our own strategic positions and options, alternative strategies to acquisitions, the range of acquisition targets, and also the target's own strategic position and options. It also entails understanding *precisely how* extra value can be added through integration or other coordination and/or change to combined operations and activities.

Having covered goals and our current strategic position, we now look briefly at gap analysis. Gap analysis helps you to see how a particular acquisition fits into your own strategic management process.

KILLER
QUESTIONS

- How strong is your own strategic position prior to becoming committed to a specific acquisition?
- What other routes to growth exist – other than to acquire a particular target?
- Is 'do nothing' or simply maintain your strategy a viable option?
- Would a share buy-back actually help you to utilize surplus capital rather than dissipating it on potentially value-destroying acquisitions?
- Will the value you hope to add to the target be reasonably easy to extract?
- What are the strategic options available to the target given its competitive position and stream of opportunities?
- What external environment changes might impact on the target or also on yourself?
- What disposal options are likely to exist in the future should you have exhausted possibilities of adding value, or be faced with better opportunities of adding value for a specific acquisition?

Gap analysis – where do acquisitions it in?

While gap analysis has been used since the 1960s (Ansoff, 1965), it has almost been forgotten about in management practise. Figure 2.2 pictures gap analysis. The vertical axis represents economic profit generation while the horizontal axis is the time dimension – usually represented as being between three to five years. Gap analysis distinguishes between:

(a) The business's prospects where there is no new development – this may be in a situation of declining economic profit.

(b) The effect of incremental, organic improvements based on current plans.

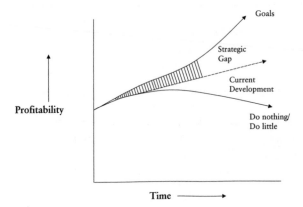

Figure 2.2 *Gap analysis.*

(c) Shareholder's (and thus management's) aspirations for the business.

(d) The gap between (a) plus (b) and (c).

Gap analysis brings the topic of acquisitions onto the management agenda, and offers the acquisition champion an excellent tool for creating real interest in their potential.

The gap (which can be defined in terms of scale, profit or economic value added – which has a focus on the future stream of net cash flows) needs to be bridged by some combination of:

• New, breakthrough organic strategies – either within existing business units or as nursery ventures

• Alliances

• Acquisitions

• Divestment or restructuring of value – diluting or destroying business.

- It gives a really clear focus, and set of expectations for an acquisition.
- It encourages debate about whether acquisitive, organic or alliance development is the most appropriate path.

While it is not necessarily easy to compose a mathematical rigour on this process, it does provide a very helpful framework for decision on future choices and trade-offs, and for understanding the role of acquisitions, specifically in generating value.

A major services PLC with turnover of over £500 million decided to draw up a revised, three-year corporate plan as part of a strategic review. Ninety per cent of its then profit (and 75% of its turnover) came from a single division – this division was a market leader in a mature, new commodity market with low profit potential. Two previous acquisitions (which represented part of a past diversification strategy) were now loss making.

The group had developed a newly expanding division in a market with good growth prospects and with less price sensitivity – mainly by organic development following an initial series of acquisitions.

The group had not formally conducted a gap analysis before. Using gap analysis (involving an evaluation of the economic profit streams of current business):

- One of the two loss-making acquisitions was sold and the other was closed (capping the ongoing loss of shareholder value).

- A nursery venture team was set up to look at new business models – this was set up separately from the organizational climate of the one division (which was focused very heavily on internal cost valuation).

- A major acquisition in the newer, growing business area was made to position this smaller division as a viable force in that market, and to add significant economic profit and to help re-rate the group on the stock market.

This group was successful in turning around its profitability and its share price.

Here gap analysis was used to examine the options and to relate these to projections of economic profit. This enabled top management to review the economic profit gap and to see what contribution acquisitions might make.

Acquisition options

This chapter helps the acquisition champion assess the options through their:

- Strategic attractiveness

- Financial attractiveness

- Implementation difficulty

- Uncertainty and risk

- Stakeholder acceptability

Winnie the Pooh – on strategic options

The book depicts a teddy bear being dragged unceremoniously down stairs. The story goes as follows:

Here is Edward Bear going down stairs, bump, bump, bump on the back of his head. It is as far as he knows the only way of coming downstairs but, sometimes he feels that there really is another way, if only he could stop bumping for a moment and think of it . . .

The morale: there are invariably other options besides doing what you have already been doing, and doing things repeatedly that do not work.

SMART QUOTES

Options / Criteria	Option 1	Option 2	Option 3	Option 4
Strategic Attractiveness				
Financial Attractiveness				
Implementation Difficulty				
Uncertainty and Risk				
Acceptability (to Stakeholders)				

Figure 2.3 The Strategic Option Grid.

Figure 2.3 explores the Strategic Option Grid, which has been used extensively for acquisition screening and appraisal. It defines some useful, generic criteria for appraising strategic options which are laid out to the left of the grid.

The detailed options (which could be acquisition, organic development or alliances), are laid out across the top.

There are four options, though the number of options can be increased if necessary. Sometimes options are created by mixing existing options (so, for example, option 3 could be a combination of option 1 and option 2). Each option will generate a different pattern of stakeholder influence, and thus of acceptability.

Each of the boxes on the strategic option grid can then be scored in terms of overall attractiveness as:

***	=	High attractiveness
**	=	Moderate attractiveness
*	=	Low attractiveness

At the bottom of the grid you then list your scores.

(Note: you will need to ensure that the two areas of 'Uncertainty and Risk' and 'Implementation Difficulty' are scored in reverse, i.e. 'Very Difficult' is scored as low attractiveness rather than as high.) Also, it is not particularly helpful to just put 'Acquisition' (or for that matter 'Alliance') at the top as a generic heading: please make this a specific target.

Figure 2.4 now explores one example of how you might use the Strategic Option Grid for an acquisition that you have already made and which is now under-performing.

	Closure	Cost cutting	Price rises	Options 2 & 3 plus more funding
	1	2	3	4
Strategic Attractiveness	***	*	**	***
Financial Attractiveness	**	**	***	***
Implementation Difficulty	*	**	*	**
Uncertainty and Risk	*	**	*	**
Stakeholder Acceptability	*	**	*	***
Total Score	8	9	8	13

Figure 2.4 Strategic Option Grid – acquisition strategy.

In Figure 2.4 option 1 (Closure) appears to be strategically and financially attractive if uncertain, difficult and less acceptable. Options 2 and 3 look marginally more attractive, but it is option 4 – to obtain more centralized funding, raise prices and cut costs – that might save the organization.

SHORT
EXERCISE

Acquisition strategy – the big picture – thinking it through

Using Figure 2.3 as an framework for reflecting on acquisition strategy:

- Does this figure highlight that you had more options than you perhaps previously imagined – and thus perhaps takes the pressure of thinking that you must desperately acquire something?

- Does this figure suggest that particular blind-spots might exist (e.g. have you thought about whether you can add more value to the target company than other potential parents are able to?)

Have you thought the strategy through dynamically: you may have thought about the present environment but what about the impact of future environmental change?

We now explore the generic criteria within the Strategic Option Grid in more depth.

Strategic attractiveness

'Strategic attractiveness' can be defined according to a number of factors including:

- Market growth (present)

- Market volatility

- Competitive intensity

An acquisition can in general be justified only if it leaves the combined enterprise stronger than the sum of the two individual enterprises. This normally means that both parties should be able to bring something to the party, in that the joint value chains of the acquiring and the acquired company be able to achieve a sustainable competitive advantage that is not easily attainable by either party separately, applies to acquisitions.

D. Faulkner and C. Bowman, *The Essence of Competitive Strategy* (1995)

- Future market growth

- Fit with own capability

- Fit to our brand

- Likely edge over competitors

- Scale of opportunity

- Focus or possible dilution of our strategy

Financial attractiveness

Financial attractiveness focuses on the key value and cost drivers which underpin a strategic option. A 'value driver' is defined as 'anything which directly or indirectly generates cash inflows, present and future, into the business' (Grundy, 1998). A 'cost driver' is defined as 'anything which directly or indirectly generates cash outflows, present and future, out of the business'.

Key criteria here could be:

- Incremental sales volumes generated

- Premium pricing achieved

The business equivalent of Catch 22 often applies. If the price is low and represents a discount on asset value, the company may be a weak one, and would represent a poor purchase, likely to absorb management time and weaken the acquirer. If the company is a good one, however, the price is likely to be corresponding high, which will mean the addition of a large amount of goodwill to the acquirer's balance sheet, and an initial decline in return on capital until some synergies can be realized and caused to feed through to profits

D. Faulkner and C. Bowman, *The Essence of Competitive Strategy* (1995)

- Discounts avoided

- Costs reduced

- Costs avoided (e.g. one head office rather than two)

- Strategy development is accelerated or retarded

- Impact on share price.

(While the final criteria – 'Impact on share price' is not strictly a cash inflow or outflow to the business, it does impact shareholder value directly.)

Implementation difficulty

Implementation difficulty needs to be anticipated *over the total time of implementation*, and not just during its early phase.

- The inherent complexity of the acquisition, or of integration plans

- Clarity of implementation strategy

- Your own determination and commitment

- Resistances (within the target)

• Availability of your resources and skills – and within the acquisition

Uncertainty and risk

Detailed factors for evaluating uncertainty and risk are diverse and specific to the context of a specific option. Some generic factors include:

• Environmental uncertainty (Will external conditions change? For example, economic and competitive conditions, new entrants, price competition/price war)

• Management uncertainty (Can we make it work?)

• Cultural uncertainty (Will people adapt?)

Stakeholder acceptability

Having worked through the previous four criteria (which typically takes managers a relatively short period of time – at least in outline), we are in better shape to examine the crucial criteria of stakeholder acceptability. Key stakeholders here include managers, directors, shareholders, staff and customers.

Setting the detailed criteria

When you have finally come up with a small list of candidates, then is the time to apply your acquisition criteria to sort out which one may be worth approaching. These criteria are best expressed as acquisition do's and don'ts, rather than as bland criteria.

Smart ways of buying a house – with criteria

- You will widen your search.
- You will be able to the trade-off advantages and disadvantages of any new property more objectively and easily.
- You will not overlook less obvious.
- You will identify 'stoppers'.

If this was for acquiring a house – why not do this for acquisitions too?

An example of criteria for an acquisition in the financial services industry is as follows:

Acquisition do's

- We must be able to negotiate a change of name (to the group).

- It must be of sufficient size (current profitability of over £5 million per annum) to be worth doing.

- It must be a leader (as benchmarked by customers) in its particular niche.

- We must be able to keep its strong management

Acquisition don'ts

- It must not be dominated by a key individual.

- The culture must not be rather different to our own . . .

- Or we will not pay over £50 million for the acquisition.

These acquisition do's and don'ts take some of the emotional heat and subjectivity out of acquisition evaluation. They will also enable the acquisition champion to help allay fears of top management that the search, screening and evaluation process has not been sufficiently rigorous.

Determining criteria – do's and don'ts

It is extremely helpful to do this from the point of view of 'do's and don'ts'. These should be spelt out *prior to* any acquisition appraisal. Consider now a more specific example – the potential acquisition of an insurance broker.

Example – from the insurance broking market

An insurance company was looking to acquire another one. Its list of do's or ('must do's') and don'ts runs like this:

Must do's

- We must be able to change the name of the company to reflect the name of our brand.

- The target must have a strong reputation rather than be a marginal player in its market.

- We must be able to add tangible value which we can capture within a two-year period, at least.

- We must be sure of keeping existing key staff.

Don'ts

- We must not be forced into giving assurances on maintaining employment continuity of all key existing directors.

- We must not pay over a price–earnings ratio of 15.

- There must not be any significant downsides to the deal discovered during due diligence.

Notice how specific these do's and don'ts are – they are not highly generic like 'strategic fit' or 'generates synergies', etc. They are – and do need to be – highly concrete and specific.

It is typically the acquisition criteria that didn't appear to fit – either in total or partially – which tend to cause subsequent problems.

Bearing this in mind, now tackle the following exercise:

SHORT
EXERCISE

Acquisition criteria – do's and don'ts

Draw up a list of acquisition do's and don'ts for screening processes for your own potential acquisition:

Acquisition do's (must do's)	Acquisition don'ts	Acquisition nice-to-haves

Detailed evaluation – external

The detailed external analysis of a target focuses on understanding the inherent attractiveness of its markets – and of its competitive position – see Figure 2.5. This can be achieved by using the GE (or General Electric) grid.

Originally devised by General Electric, the GE grid answers the questions of

• Which businesses are in the most inherently attractive markets?

• What businesses have the strongest competitive positions?

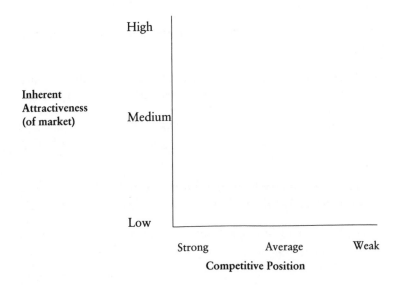

Figure 2.5 "GE" (General Electric) grid.

Ideally, you would wish your business (existing and acquisitions) to be *both* inherently attractive markets *and* have very strong competitive positions.

An example of a GE grid is shown in Figure 2.5, with inherent market attractiveness being pictured vertically, and relative competitive position horizontally.

The GE grid is used for a number of applications relevant to acquisitions;

1. To get a better fix on your own strategic position first, as a prelude to looking at acquisitions and other options. This is split down by product/market segment.

2. To analyse and evaluate the strategic position of a target acquisition, and especially:

    – To compare and contrast it *vis-à-vis* your own strategic position. Is there overall consistency between both business portfolios?

    – To explore whether acquisition integration can materially reposition any of these businesses particularly in terms of relative competitive position.

    – To understand the basis of economic profit generation in target's business, and to challenge whether this is likely to be sustainable.

    – To understand how much effort in integration and investment may be required to reposition the required business in order to improve its economic profit.

3. To examine options for which parts of the target it might be appropriate to dispose of or close.

4. To track the strategic position of the acquisition following a deal: is it really living up to its expectations or did we fundamentally mis-read its strategic position?

The GE grid is the best way of probing assumed 'strategic attractiveness' in the strategic option grid which we saw in the earlier section on 'Op-tions' (see Figure 2.3). Indeed, when we use the GE grid we may well need to go another level of analysis down – to set criteria for inherent market attractiveness and for 'competitive position'. We will go into this in greater depth in Chapter 4, but for the time being we can assume that 'inherent market attractiveness' means:

- Growth rate (see 'growth driver analysis' – in Chapter 4)

- Competitive pressure (see the 'Five competitive forces' – in Chapter 4)

- Environmental volatility (see the 'PEST factors' in Chapter 4)

'Competitive advantage' can now be defined as meaning either

- Higher customer value added (real and /or perceived) *vis-à-vis* com-petitors: as seen from a customer perspective (and not ours) – (see customer value analysis in Chapter 4)

- Lower unit cost levels *vis-à-vis* competitors (see strategic cost target-ing in Chapter 4)

The significance of the positions on the GE grid means (in broad terms):

- North-west positions: a very major long-term generator of economic profit.

- South-west positions: a significant long-term generator of economic growth – but with constant struggle.

- North-east positions: a marginal long-term generator of economic profit.

- Due south positions: a mixture between just break-way even in economic profit and some economic profit dilution.

- South-east positions: significant if not major shareholder value destruction.

A step-by-step worked example for the GE grid is now taken from a now classic M&A case study: the acquisition of Rover Group by BMW.

BMW and Rover case study

BMW's strategic position – 1994

BMW was a very successful family-owned company which has exploited important niches in the car market with a strong differentiation strategy. Originally renowned for its quality motorcycles, after Second World War it diversified into small cars. Although once regarded as the poor neighbour of Mercedes, BMW had actually reached a position on a par with (and some would say ahead of) Mercedes. In late 1994 BMW displaced Mercedes as the supplier of engines to the next generation of Rolls-Royce cars.

BMW had built a very impressive brand by 1994. This was established by very clear market positioning, a very high-quality product and service from its dealer network to match. The very success of BMW meant, however, that it had become a prime target for competitors to emulate, possibly by moving into direct attack.

BMW's strategic position in 1994 was relatively strong, with its very strong marque, premium prices, dealer network and its relative quality levels. But was BMW (as of the mid-1990s) capable of sustaining its competitive position against competition from both Western and Far Eastern sources (such as from Toyota's Lexus)? There were some symptoms that led to a turning point in BMW's strategic health around the early 1990s.

First, BMW's reputation for quality suffered: certain of the early 3 series models in the early 1990s had significant quality problems.

But besides the increasing threat of competition, BMW was moving in the direction of medium and smaller sizes, and was even (as of 1994) contemplating launching its own '2' series (organic development). Although BMW sold a lot more 3 series than 5 series, and a lot more 5 series than 7 series, it was actually the top-of-the-range cars that are rated as outstanding by motor magazines. So was this a move to downsize a strategic temptation that would ultimately weaken BMW? Also, the competitive forces traditionally tended to be more acutely adverse when one considered the volume end of the car market.

But even before BMW had actively considered buying Rover it had decided to experiment (besides considering a '2' series) with the smaller end of medium-sized cars with its BMW Compact, launched in 1994. So BMW *did* have at least two organic options to its acquisitive strategy for Rover Group, at around 1994. Summarizing the company's strategic position as at 1994, BMW:

- had been (and still was) a very successful company which had achieved market leadership in executive, high-performance cars in Europe;

- had a worldwide reputation for quality which is now being imitated by a variety of players;

- had a product line which was beginning to appear out of fit with the changing market environment, and which appeared somewhat limited and perhaps over-focused.

But does it actually follow from this that BMW should buy Rover Group. It is now worthwhile for you (the reader) to spend some time pondering what other options were available to BMW.

SHORT
EXERCISE

BMW strategic options

What options were available to BMW (as at 1994) – other than to acquire Rover as a central plank of its strategic development – and how attractive are these? You may wish to explore, for instance:

- Strategic alliances.
- Organic development (of new products) to broaden its range.
- Other acquisition options.
- Specific migration of its competitive strategy to have less emphasis (or even more emphasis) on differentiation.
- Maintaining and protecting its current niche position.
- Exploiting new technologies for engine and vehicle design.

Specific options that you might have come up with are: acquire Porsche, acquire Volvo, merge with VW Audi, a partnership with VW Audi, set up its own four-wheel-drive business, apply its engine technology into other markets (like boats, public transport). It could also have pursued organic development with a BMW 2 series, a four-wheel-drive car, a people mover or a further exclusive sports car.

Having analysed BMW with considerable depth, we now turn to Rover Group.

Rover's strategic position – 1994

Following a very difficult history in public ownership and one beset with huge losses, Mrs Thatcher's government sought to sell off the Rover Group in the late 1980s. The Rover Group was the rebadged bundle of businesses formerly part of the BL (or British Leyland Group). At this point – and continuing into the future – the Group suffered from under-investment, lack of economics of scale, poor quality and poor image, and poor labour productivity.

The Conservative government clearly wanted to privatize Rover but for obvious political reasons did not want it to fall into foreign ownership. A deal crystallized with British Aerospace (BAe), which on purely financial grounds was rather favourable. BAe acquired Rover for around £150 million in 1988.

Rover had sought to reposition itself during the period 1985–1993 and a big part of this success was attributable to the involvement of Honda which supplied Rover's key engines. Honda had taken a 20 per cent stake in Rover Group, and this strategic alliance appeared to be working very well. Honda began to see Rover as a central plank of its European strategy.

The Honda connection enabled Rover to tap into Honda's technology economies of scale. Rover was thus able to reach economic sustainability at a smaller size than if it had been completely independent. The Honda link came at a price, however, as Honda's bargaining power enabled Honda to extract value out of the relationship through its technology licensing arrangement, making Rover less profitable.

But the second and third major planks of Rover's attempted strategic turnaround were to reposition its product range to become much higher quality and also through productivity breakthrough.

In terms of products, Rover had previously had a product mishmash with large executive cars alongside the Maestro, Allegro, Metro and Mini. In the earlier 1980s Rover appeared to be trying to be a broad-based provider (with some niches) and simultaneously pursuing differentiation and lower-cost strategies. Rover (then BL) had made the mistake of being 'stuck in the middle' without a (then) clear competitive position.

But from this very weak position in the mid-1980s, Rover sought to:

• Move up-market; and

• Have a much tighter focus on its car range.

The product range improvements made by Rover (prior to BMW's acquisition) included:

• The launch of the 200 and 400 series to gradually supplant and replace the Allegro and Maestro.

• The 600 series – which was built on an identical platform to the Honda Accord, and commanded a price premium.

• The huge success of the fashionable Discovery range of four-wheel-drive cars.

• The rebadging of the Metro as the Rover 100 in late 1994, backed up with an advertising campaign to attempt to give the car a feel of style (moving it from the 'grey-market' – the over-50s – to a younger market).

• A restored reputation for reliability.

- The partially restored marque of Rover.

- Its somewhat improved product range (in some areas)

But offsetting these relatively fragile sources of competitive advantage we can also identify:

- Its relatively small size and dependence on Honda technology.

- The need for investment on a scale that was difficult to finance through internal cash generation.

- Its high unit costs.

According to *The Sunday Times* (6 February 1994), Rover also paid Honda substantial suns for the car floorplans and the engines for its larger models – plus a royalty for each jointly developed car Rover sold. This agreement barred Rover from selling Honda-based models in markets Honda wanted for itself. So Rover was not allowed to sell the 600 in America (and so this option was also precluded for any acquirer).

The Sunday Times went on to say that Rover was caught in a Honda bear-hug: while Honda gave the British company protection, it prevented Rover's cars from breaking into real profit. The Rover–Honda strategic alliances underscores the risks that any medium or smaller-sized player exposes itself to when joining a strategic alliance with a larger and more powerful partner.

Rover's sales were still (in the 1990s) predominantly concentrated in the UK. Also, outside the UK its models had very low market share (even in continental Europe) and were sometimes not known at all.

So, overall, in 1994 Rover's competitive position was still fragile. Outside the UK its brand was weak, its market share was low and it lacked a strong distribution network. Its parent, British Aerospace, was no longer fed by an entrepreneurial visionary, eager to develop an industrial conglomerate, but by an ex-BTR, financially hard-nosed chartered accountant. Under the terms of the government's deal with BAe, Rover could not be sold for five years; once this period expired, the scene was set for the sale of Rover.

Given BAe's reluctance to continue as Rover's parent, Rover was left with a number of strategic options. Simpson (the Chairman of Rover) concluded that there were two options:

- A full take-over by Honda

- A management buyout

Honda, at the time, seemed disinterested in Rover as a fully-owned subsidiary and a buyout looked impossible to finance (given Rover's thirst for capital – present and future – and its low rate of profit, which was woefully short of that required by venture capital).

Only Mercedes and BMW were likely candidates: the third option, Volkswagen, was still struggling to digest its late 1980s growth. So BAe turned to BMW for the strategic rescue of Rover Group. But if one had been BMW what sense would it have made to acquire Rover Group if one had applied the GE grid?

To get a better idea of Rover's strategic position, let us therefore look at the product/marketing positioning of the Group. To achieve this we will position Rover's products on the GE grid. This maps products–markets in terms of their inherent attractiveness – which is a function of:

- vulnerability to PEST factors (or political, economic, social and technological factors);

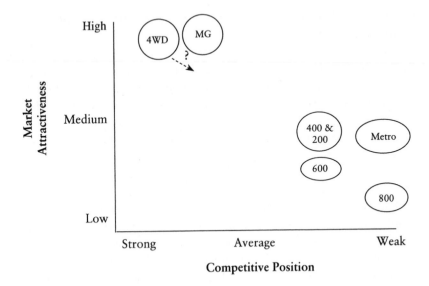

Figure 2.6 GE grid – Rover Group, 1994.

- the rate of sustainable market growth; and

- Porter's five competitive forces (1980) (which include the bargaining power of buyers, suppliers, competitive rivalry and the threat of new entrants or of substitutes).

On the horizontal axis we plot relative competitive position, factoring in here Rover's relative value-added (to customers) and Rover's unit costs relative to competitors.

Figure 2.6 now uses the GE grid (as of 1994) to analyse Rover's product–market niches. The 600 series is shown as being pushed to the right due to advancing competitive position. The 800 series is also weakly positioned. (BMW's position was much more favourable, being in the north-west of the grid.)

By contrast, the Rover 400 and 200 and Metro niches were in marginally more attractive markets (due to the assumed trend by customers to fewer, smaller cars) although with weak competitive positions. The Metro and Mini are not seen as competitively strong and the Mini in particular is depicted (without new investment) as being dangerously close to the brink.

The overall profile of Rover's portfolio (apart from the four-wheel-drive division, which is undisputedly in the north-west), is weak. Put simply, this analysis cried out for massive new investment. And this huge requirement was one of the big factors which blew BMW's integration plans off course. Even with the four-wheel-drive division, competitive rivalry was increasing rapidly – and even this division was vulnerable to fashion and environmental factors (the Discovery is hardly a small, environmentally friendly car).

A substantial part of Rover's current profits were reputed to be earned by the Discovery alone, so concerns on this score were important. Clearly BMW was banking on the growth drivers for four-wheel-drive winning out – as penetration of Europe is only 2.5 per cent (compared to 10 per cent in the United States) there was still a belief that growth would win out.

Now turning to parallels with your own acquisition situation, try out the following exercise:

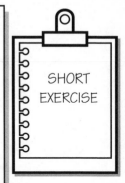

SHORT
EXERCISE

Detailed evaluation – internal

Although we will be going into more depth on the internal evaluation in Chapter 4, the following overall key factors are important:

- What are the detailed competitive strengths of particular products or services?

- What are the strengths and weaknesses of underlying processes and systems?

- How are the key drivers of costs being managed?

- How flexible are organizational structures?

- What is the culture and mind-set of the organization?

- What (if any) are its distinctive technologies as other scarce competencies?

- Does the company have any other strategic assets that are hard for other companies to replicate or imitate?

- How dependent is the organization on particularly important or scarce skills (such as top management, IT or other technology), or key account relationships?

- What are the strengths and weaknesses and vulnerabilities of the organization's supply base?

Reader exercise: for a potential acquisition of your choice, apply the above key questions as part of the internal evaluation of a target's future strategy.

Process considerations

This short subsection deals with the most important process implications involved in developing an acquisition strategy.

As we will see in the next chapter, it is essential to involve the management team whose primary responsibility will be to integrate the acquisition. Unless this occurs there is a very real risk that ownership of the acquisition strategy and the commitment to the acquisition will be severely diluted.

Also, it is highly advisable (even before detailed due diligence) to collect some initial data on the target. This is required both to support and challenge the analysis of the inherent attractiveness of the markets which its business are in, and to evaluate its competitive positioning – product–market by product market. This might entail some:

- Review of commentary on industry trends generally.

- Customer data collection – to check out that the company's products are as competitively strong as has been thought or assumed, and any perceptions concerning their product lifecycle characteristics.

- Selected competitor analysis – in order to get a better fix on relative competitive position.

In order to achieve this process with least effort and cost, and with maximum value it is suggested that:

- You conduct the preliminary analysis using the GE grid, supported, as necessary with the analysis and techniques from the next chapter – for example understanding the growth drivers impacting on the company also its level of competitive pressure (Porter's five competitive forces) – for determining inherent market attractiveness.

- You then define the issues and assumptions which underpin this acquisition which are both:

  - most important, and

  - most uncertain.

- You then formulate a number of key questions (which are very focused) that you need to have answered.

- For each question you look at the options for answering the question with ease, value and low cost, and the most cunning way of answering these.

The above process should help to telescope the process into a couple of days rather than weeks. It should also provide better pointers for your more detailed due-diligence process (which can otherwise become a data-collection process that is almost an end in itself).

Summary

Developing an effective acquisitions strategy is an absolutely crucial part of the process. Unless this is carried out effectively, not only can you miss major downsides, but you may end up acquiring the wrong target.

Developing a successful and robust acquisition strategy needs to begin by defining as our strategic position and plans for development (some of which may be acquisition, some may include acquisition, and some may not even involve acquisition). Using the strategic option grid, one should be able to narrow down the focus of lines of enquiry.

Then by setting the 'acquisition do's and don'ts' – those specific criteria for deciding whether an acquisition target is prima-facie worthwhile investigating –it is possible to avoid getting carried away with the thrill of the chase – at least at this early stage.

Once one has narrowed down the options to one or more targets, it is then appropriate to examine the target's strategic position, you should then use the acquisition do's and don'ts to help you to perform a health-check in order to evaluate how the target will really fit into corporate goals and into enhancing our own strategic position. At a more detailed level the GE grid then provides a more bottom-up view of its strategic attractiveness which you then proceed to check out in the next chapter.

3

Search

Introduction

Assuming that you as acquisition champion now have a robust acquisition in place, it is now time to think about how to mobilize your team and begin the search.

Mobilization requires some careful thinking through, particularly because of the issue of ownership of the idea of making the acquisition. This is especially important where a group of companies is making an

> The acquisition-led approach is seductive, and it is easy for the wannabe acquirer to think that all that is necessary for success are a few ideas and the phone numbers of good firms of consultants and investment bankers. In these circumstances, everyone will want to do a deal, be it good, bad or indifferent, and at any price that can be funded. Remember that the road to hell is paved with good advisers.
>
> R. Koch, *The Financial Times Guide to Strategy*

SMART QUOTES

acquisition and its corporate centre is the prime mover in initiating the acquisition. Unless the business or division that will be involved in integrating the business is fully involved at the outset, major difficulties in subsequent ownership can occur.

While the suggestion that this might happen may seem far-fetched – and be met with incredulity, this can be a very real issue, as we see in the following case study.

Make-It-All plc

Some years ago a major public limited company, which we will call MIA (or "Make-It-All" plc), was making an aggressive acquisition of manufacturing businesses. One day the Chief Executive of its biggest division had a telephone call from the Group Chief Executive which ran more or less like this:

"Bill, I have just got some very exciting news for you. Our 'A' team (the Acquisitions team) has successfully negotiated in principle to buy an exciting new in-fill company for your discussion."

At the end of the telephone there was just stunned silence. The Divisional Chief Executive was quickly playing his options through his mind: should he cancel his forthcoming holiday in the Caribbean? Should he take that job the head-hunter had propositioned him with? Or should he question the logic of acquiring that particular business?

The above brief example highlights just how quickly things go wrong even when there was no devious intent. Clearly, an alternative approach within a group structure would be to have the business unit or the division looking out for acquisition opportunities. This would realize a number of advantages, particularly:

- Local management would be more actively involved in identifying and screening acquisition opportunities.

- These opportunities would be more likely to fit in with the needs of the business.

- Ownership would be much greater – and thus local motivation to make acquisition integration work.

On the downside, decentralizing the search process could produce a number of disadvantages, including:

- Decentralization would almost certainly be more costly as local staff would not get up the learning curve as far as a specialist, central team.

- They might also make more mistakes.

- And be more difficult to co-ordinate centrally.

- And would be closer to their own pet projects – and be less able to maintain objectivity.

- And also miss opportunities that make sense more in group terms, rather than from the narrower perspective of a particular strategic business unit.

Smart ways of co-ordinating acquisition resource should therefore include:

- Disseminate best practice in the acquisition process, including strategy-making screening, deal-making and integration.

- Co-ordinate the inputs from specialist head office staff centrally in finance, tax, legal, pensions, etc., and from external professional advisers.

- Proactively seek out potential targets for divisions/business centrally – but based on divisional/business strategies – rather than opportunistically. (The core management responsibility for preparing a potential target lies still with the business, and not with the centre.)

Mobilization is not only about setting up or becoming part of the acquisitions team, however; it is about deploying sufficient time resource. Acquisitions are very time-consuming projects, and this can easily become a full-time job. It may well be essential to appoint a business unit manager as the full-time project manager – probably as a secondment.

Having covered mobilization, let us now turn to the role of acquisition search. This takes us through:

- Sources of target

- Approaching the target

in the next section.

Different search processes

The word 'search' could be taken to mean the process of exploring opportunities in both likely and less likely places in order to meet your objectives. This process of exploring opportunities can be structured or less-structured, it can be deliberate or accidental, ongoing or spasmodic.

Successful acquirers in the past (like Hanson plc) tended to be more structured (rather than less), more deliberate (rather than accidental) and more relentless (rather than spasmodic) in their search.

The careful specification of acquisition criteria (which we discussed earlier) will help in providing more focus finding the optimal acquisition target. The development of an effective acquisition strategy generally *will* also weed out these areas of *where not to look.*

Indeed, the very notion of a less-structured search in itself should give rise to concern. For it is hardly likely that one will come up with an acquisition which has a clear strategic *logic that is not known to you already.*

If you are going so far out of your product/market/core competence domain that you do not know your target at all (or even relatively well), then this should ring major alarm bells. Equally, if you are to enter a new geographic region that you do not know very well, then this will clearly amplify risks.

Moving now onto sources of target, these might include two main types:

- Market, competitive and competitor analysis

- Financial brokers including merchant banks and accountants

Market, competitive and competitor analysis

As we outlined in the earlier section on acquisition strategy, market and competitive analysis can help to tease out specific acquisition targets. For example, this can help you to identify:

- Suppliers to potentially acquire (through backward integration)

- Distribution channels (or perhaps even customers) who might be advantageous to acquire

- Acquisition targets in different geographic markets

> Smart
> things to say
> about competitor
> analysis

Analysing a competitor can frequently lead to an alliance, possible leading to a successful acquisition or just doing this directly.

Financial brokers

Financial brokers include merchant banks, accountants and other intermediates. These range from those who maintain an ongoing database of companies who might be available for sale to ones who just might happen to have knowledge of companies who are for sale. (Accountant-only firms tend to fall into the latter category.)

Merchant banks (and other brokers) may not always provide the trouble-free route to finding a suitable acquisition target that you are looking for. First, they will obviously have their database of companies who are potentially up for sale. These may or may not map onto your own acquisition strategy and criteria. Where you lack a clear acquisition strategy and criteria using this channel as the primary source of acquisition target this could be potentially blinkered and dangerous.

While they might also come up with suggestions for them to approach on a more proactive basis, this again will be dependent upon the quality and orientation of their contacts. Very quickly, this route might channel you in the direction of targets who may not fit your strategy and acquisition criteria particularly well. Merchant banks and other acquisition brokers can also be expensive in fee terms – which means that while hopefully you get excellent advice, you are adding to transaction costs.

There is therefore probably no better substitute for yourselves being the prime driver of acquisition search, rather than relying upon third parties as the primary (or even secondary) route to find an acquisition candidate. (This assumes you have the competences necessary to conduct the search process effectively.)

Approaching your target

Approaching the target is often viewed with concern by management of the acquirer. Thoughts that are often in the minds of the acquiring managers are: 'Perhaps we will be asked outright as to what we are prepared to pay, and if we react to this, this might jeopardize our negotiating position.' Or 'Just how do I approach this subject – and say why I am calling?' Or 'What happens if they really do not want to sell – and actually get quite unpleasant about the approach.'

Although it is not possible to prescribe generally as to what the best way of approaching a specific target will be, here are some suggestions:

- Who might be the person who would most naturally expect the telephone call to be made to? Is this likely to be the Chief Executive, the Chairman, an influential major holder of shares, or a key non-executive director.

- Find out more about the individuals who might be key stakeholders in any division to sell. Who is likely to have most influence upon the division? What is likely to be on their agendas?

- Are there any ways of conveniently arranging for a chance meeting to happen – for example at an industry conference?

- Where the target company has been known in the past to have con-

SMART QUOTES

The financial institutions work only for one client – for themselves.

Chief executive of an entertainment company

templated selling the business, then alluding to this fact can be used to hint at the purpose of the conversation.

Any manager on the receiving end of such a call will need to deal with:

• The initial surprise – perhaps even shock.

• Thinking about whether they would actually like to be acquired by this particular company – and working with its management team.

• Thinking through their own personal agendas – which might include the value of any shares or stock options, and the likelihood of having to leave the company following integration, what it will be like to work under a new ownership.

• Thinking through its commercial logic.

• Anticipating the reactions of colleagues – and shareholders.

An informal setting on neutral ground is ideal for a first meeting. A quiet hotel where discussions are less likely to be overheard by others is likely to offer a good venue.

Most probably this would mean a meeting of two people each from both parties to build ownership for a potential deal, and also to facilitate the decision-making process. (Many managers like to have another team member there to act as a sounding board.)

Deal-making considerations

Approaching the target can lead to signals being given by senior representatives of the acquirer which might prejudice a fair deal. One of the disadvantages of a relaxed meeting (as we outlined on the previous sub-section) is that it can become *too* relaxed and *too* friendly – it does still need to be business-like.

Summary

Mobilization for the acquisition requires considerable planning and co-ordination. This planning should cover: who will play what roles in the acquisition both within the business unit and at any corporate centre; and also, who will be central to be a part of the acquisition project team and at what phase they should be involved.

'Search' should not be carried too far as a 'driving part of the process'. Unless you are already familiar with the acquisition target – even if this is without having some in-depth knowledge – it is not so likely that this target will have real strategic fit. Equally, merchant banks and other intermediaries might yield fruitful acquisition candidates, but this is very hit and miss.

Approaching the target is a highly sensitive area, but pointers to how to do this include careful selection of which stakeholder to approach and understanding their potential agendas. A 'softer' approach – rather than one which is very direct can be more helpful.

When making initial contact it is crucial not to set expectations which cannot be delivered during detailed negotiations.

4

Acquisitions – Strategic Due Diligence

Introduction

Acquisition attractiveness can be assessed, as we have already seen, with the Strategic Option Grid. But now we need to consider in more detail how we should appraise the five key criteria of:

- Strategic attractiveness

- Financial attractiveness

- Implementation difficulty

- Uncertainty and risk

- Stakeholder acceptability

In the next five sections we go through these criteria in more depth, particularly how you can use some 'bottom-up' techniques for understanding them.

Evaluating strategic attractiveness – the 'GE' grid

The detailed external analysis of a target focuses on understanding the inherent attractiveness of its markets – and of its competitive position. This can be achieved by using the GE (or General Electric) grid, which we saw earlier.

Originally devised by General Electric, the GE grid answers two questions:

• Which businesses are in the most inherently attractive markets?

• What businesses have the strongest competitive positions?

Ideally, you would wish your business (existing and acquisitions) to be *both* inherently attractive markets *and* have very strong competitive positions.

The GE grid is shown once again in Figure 4.1, with inherent market attractiveness being pictured vertically, and relative competitive position horizontally.

The GE grid is used by the acquisition champion for a number of applications relevant to acquisitions:

1. To get a better fix on your own strategic position first, as a prelude to looking at acquisitions and other options. This is then split down by product/market segment.

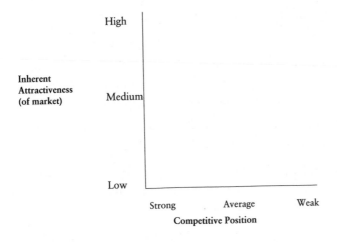

High

Inherent
Attractiveness
(of market)

Medium

Low

Strong　　　　　　　Average　　　　　Weak

Competitive Position

Figure 4.1 General Electric (GE) grid.

- It position targets businesses both externally and internally – and visually.
- It helps stop you from paying excessive premiums.
- It helps target, and cost–benefit analyse, integration and development strategies.

Smart things about the GE grid

2. To analyse and evaluate the strategic position of a target acquisition, and specially:

 - To compare and contrast it *vis-à-vis* your own strategic position. Is there overall consistency between both business portfolios?

 - To explore whether acquisition integration can materially reposition any of these businesses, particularly in terms of relative competitive position.

- To understand the basis of economic profit generation in target's business, and to challenge whether this is likely to be sustainable.

- To understand how much effort in integration and investment may be required to reposition the required business in order to improve its economic profit.

3. To examine options for which parts of the target it might be appropriate to dispose of or close.

4. To track the strategic position of the acquisition following a deal: is it really living up to its expectations or did we fundamentally misread its strategic position?

The GE grid is the best way of the acquisition champion probing assumed 'strategic attractiveness' in the strategic option grid which we saw in the central section on 'Options'. Indeed, when we use the GE grid we may well need to go another level of analysis down – to set criteria for inherent market attractiveness and for 'competitive position'. We will go into this in greater depth in our Chapter 5 on due diligence, but for the time being we can assume that 'inherent market attractiveness' means:

- Growth rate

- Competitive pressure

- Environmental volatility

'Competitive pressure' here means the relative bargaining power of the buyers, the suppliers, and the degree of rivalry between competitors.

'Competitive advantage' here means, either

- Higher customer value added (real and /or perceived) *vis-à-vis* competitors: as seen from a customer perspective (and not ours) – (see customer value analysis later in this chapter)

- Lower unit cost levels *vis-à-vis* competitors (see strategic cost targeting later in this chapter)

As we saw earlier, the significance of the positions on the GE grid means (in broad terms):

- North-west positions: a very major generator of economic profit.

- South-west positions: a significant generator of economic growth – but with constant struggle.

- North-east positions: a marginal generator of economic profit.

- Due south positions: a mixture between just break-way even in economic profit and some economic profit dilution.

- South-east positions: significant if not major shareholder value distribution.

Financial attractiveness

The financial attractiveness of an acquisition option can be evaluated by understanding its key performance drivers. A 'performance driver' can be defined as: *an external, or internal factor that is either generating superior profitability (the performance driver) or producing inferior profitability (the performance brake.*

Typical external performance drivers/brakes are:

- The rate of growth.

- The competitive pressure in an industry, which includes:

- the bargaining power of buyers

- the bargaining power of suppliers

- the level of competitive rivalry

- the entry barriers (high is good news, low is bad news)

- the threat of substitutes

• Knock-on events from adjacent industries either up stream (supplier industries) or downstream (to the ultimate consumer) or in adjacent markets.

• The mind-set of the industry: is it one where transactions tend to become increasingly a commodity, or is there a high element of emotional activity surrounding the buyer's decision.

• The impact of 'PEST' factors or political economic, social and technological factors

• Changes in the distribution chain (which might shorten it, or make it increasingly complex, difficult and costly to sell through).

• The availability of technological or other means of innovation to drive costs down

Typical internal performance drivers/brakes include:

• Brand strength

• Customer focus/service

• Relative product quality

• Product or process innovation

• Internal flexibility and speed

• Management's commercial capability

- Lower costs through economies of scale, or clever cost management

- Cultural attitudes

- Leadership

- Availability and appropriateness of new investment

- Degree of clarity in strategic focus

- Quality of operational decision-making.

To appraise financial effectiveness it is usually helpful to look at this, using a vector type format (Lewin). An example of a prioritized performance driver analysis (done by the author in 1994) is shown in Figure 4.2 for the Rover Group.

The balance of the various performance drivers (here presumed to be post-acquisition) was negative, implying that the prognosis for Rover's future financial performance was not good at all. Put simply, it suggests

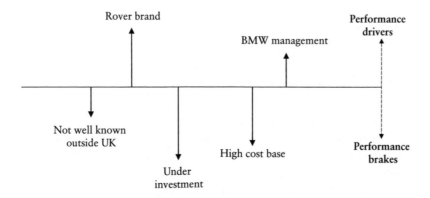

Figure 4.2 Rover performance drivers, 1995.

that apart from the four-wheel drive division, Rover's financial performance was likely to be weak.

In fact, Figure 4.2 was relatively optimistic. Missing from these performance drivers were:

- The potential impact of a very strong UK exchange rate. (This contributed to about half of Rover's 1999 losses of approximately £900 million.)

- The effect of intensified competition in the late 1990s.

- The likelihood that instead of adding to Rover's brands, BMW's managers would actually (and inadvertently) weaken it – through latest model launches.

Figure 4.2 should be performed as a useful health-check on the assumed financial performance of a target (after acquisition) Figure 4.2 should also be used to identify the areas where we will need to collect new data – in order to do the financial numbers), and also as a pre-acquisition diagnostic technique.

Evaluating implementation difficulty

In Chapter 8 we will examine a detailed way of diagnosing implementation difficulty. This will be done with force field analysis – from its original context. This analysis is performed by using a vector-picture in a similar format to Figure 4.2. The only real difference here is that instead of plotting performance drivers as vertical, upward arrows and performance drivers as downward arrows we will substitute these with (a) enabling forces (things that will make the acquisition easier to integrate, versus (b) constraining forces (things that will make it more difficult to integrate).

Uncertainty and risk

Uncertainty and risk can be dealt with using the importance–uncertainty grid (see Figure 4.3), which we also explore in Chapter 6. This plots a selected number of the key assumptions that underly on acquisition's success.

These assumptions are framed in terms of the world going right, and not the world going wrong. For instance an assumption might be: *We will be able to integrate operations so that they operate smoothly and effectively by the time the initial fifteen-month period is up.*

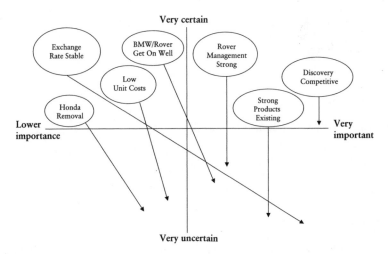

Figure 4.3

Figure 4.3 gives an example based on the Rover acquisition. This suggests that a number of key assumptions are *both* uncertain *and* important. These might include, for example:

• Rover and BMW management will co-operate well.

• Rover's unit costs are low.

• Investment requirements will not excess £400 million per annum, after acquisition.

Slightly less important and uncertain are assumptions like:

• The Rover 200 and 400 models will be successful.

Key areas of uncertainty and risk can be broken down into:

Environmental

• Regulatory changes

• Economic slow-down

• Adverse media commentary

• Anti-competitive regulatory bodies

• Consumer change in tastes, and demographics

Competitive

• New entrants

• Pending price war

• Acquisitions by other major players, reducing relative market share

• Adverse changes in distribution methods

- Customer reaction to the acquisition – taking their business elsewhere

- Competitive positioning of products shifting

- Product lifecycles – making

Operational

- Quality problems crystallizing

- More investment required than was anticipated

- Operations prove to be too complex to integrate

Organizational

- Key managers/staff leaving

- Integration takes a lot longer operationally then expected

- Cultural resistances

- Earn-out arrangements inhibit change – where old owner/manger is kept on – for a transitional period

Financial

- Current financial accounts have inflated profitability

- Inflated balance sheet assets/unexpected write-downs

- Undisclosed liabilities

- Losses through adverse foreign exchange movements

- Management accounting system is inadequate

- Financial management staff are not of assumed quality and need urgent replacing

Legal

- Title to assets is disputed

- Claims pending against the company

- Unforeseen pension fund obligatories etc.

Notice how the main risks and uncertainties covered in traditional due diligence are (in order of prioritization):

- Legal

- Financial

- Organizational

- Operational

with competitive and environmental often coming as the lowest priority. This imbalance can be remedied (at least in part) by using the Strategic Option Grid, to you as a 'bird's eye' view of this acquisition. The Grid also gives us a comparative dimension – against other possible acquisition targets, and also alliances and organic development.

Stakeholder acceptability

Stakeholder acceptability covers not just the decision-makers, but also other players with a direct or indirect influence on the acquisition.

Stakeholders also include those individuals (and groups) who might be involved either as the integrators, or even as the victims of the acquisition.

External stakeholders include customers, suppliers, regulators and the media, and potentially wider government bodies. These stakeholders will have variable influence depending upon the acquisition context.

One way of doing a stakeholder analysis is to draw up a 'Stakeholder Agenda Analysis' for a particular group of individuals, e.g. for the Directors of the acquiring company (see Figure 4.4).

This figure shows the 'turn-ons' as upward vertical vectors (or arrows), and the 'turn-offs' as downward vectors. The balance of these forces or vectors gives the group a good feel for:

• the strength of their desire to acquire;

• the reasons for that desire;

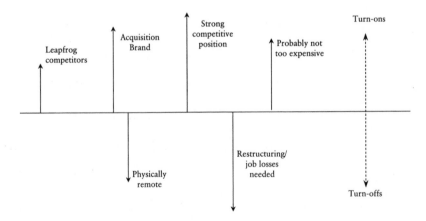

Figure 4.4 Stakeholder and agenda analysis.

- the concerns about it (the downward lines)

as a decision –making tool.

Conclusion

Strategic due diligence should be used to test out whether an acquisition is worthwhile more detailed due diligence. The Strategic Option Grid is an excellent (and proven) way to evaluate acquisition options – either as stand-alone possibilities, or as a set of different acquisition alternatives, or *vis-à-vis* alliances and organic development.

KILLER
QUESTIONS

- What are the detailed competitive strengths of particular products or services?
- What are the strengths and weaknesses of underlying processes and systems?
- How are the key drivers of costs being managed?
- How flexible are organizational structures?
- What is the culture and mind-set of the organization?
- What (if any) are its distinctive technologies as other scarce competencies?
- Does the company have any other strategic assets which are hard for other companies to replicate or imitate?
- How dependent is the organization on particularly important or scarce skills (such as top management, IT, or other technology), or key account relationships?
- What are the strengths and weaknesses and vulnerabilities of the organization's supply base?

Coupled with the bottom-up techniques of the GE grid, performance drivers, force field analysis, the uncertainty grid and stakeholder analysis, the grid is a formidable tool for helping provide management focus and objectivity.

Summary

Developing an effective acquisitions strategy is an absolutely crucial part of the process.

Unless this is carried out effectively, not only can you miss major downsides, but you may end up acquiring the wrong acquisition target anyway.

Developing a successful and robust acquisition strategy needs to begin by defining our strategic position and plans for development (some of which may be acquisition, some may include acquisition, and some may not even involve acquisition). Using the Strategic Option Grid one should be able to narrow down the focus of lines of enquiry.

Then by setting the 'acquisition do's and don'ts' – those specific criteria for deciding whether an acquisition target is prima-facie worthwhile investigating – one is perhaps somewhat less prone to getting carried away with the thrill of the chase – at least at this early stage.

Once one has narrowed down the options to one or more targets it is then appropriate to examine the target's strategic position, you should then use the acquisition do's and don'ts to help you to perform a health-check in order to evaluate how the target will really fit into corporate goals and into enhancing our own strategic position. At a more detailed level the GE grid then provides a more bottom-up view of its strategic attractiveness which you then proceed to check out in the later chapter on Evaluation (pp. 125–158).

5

Gaining the Overview – Success in Due Diligence

Introduction

'Due diligence' is defined as *the process of detailed evaluation of an acquisition to ensure that you are actually getting what you think you are getting and that there are no hidden and unexpected downsides.*

Due diligence has many legalistic connections. Obviously the legal

'Due diligence' always reminds me of Lieutenant Columbo, who always pursued his subjects with appalling doggedness, no question being too silly. *An acquisitions expert*	SMART QUOTES

SMART QUOTES

They [successful acquirers] look for *profit improvement potential of a specific nature*. For example, if the industry return on sales averages 10 per cent, and the target bumps along at 3 per cent, the predator becomes interested. He then looks to see if there is any reason (such as a weak market share position) that could explain the discrepancy. If not, he looks further, talking to people in the industry to see how far return on sales could be raised.

R. Koch, *The Financial Times Guide to Strategy*

aspects of due diligence are very important and comprise a large part of the due diligence process. But there are equally important non-legal aspects and perspectives on due diligence, particularly:

• Markets and marketing

• Products and services

• Technology

• Organization and people

The previous chapter on acquisition strategy should give you many clues as to what to focus on during non-legal due diligence. This section now helps you as acquisition champion to go to the next level of detail. Here it is just as important to link detailed due diligence back to the bigger picture, as it is to cover the above headings currently interrelating the perspectives above, depicted in Figure 5.1.

Detailed performance diagnosis

In this chapter we consider:

• Markets and marketing

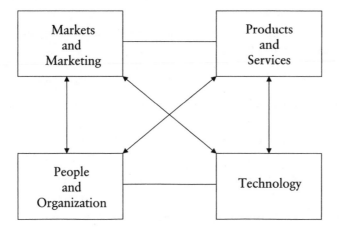

Figure 5.1 Integrating perspectives in due diligence.

READER EXERCISE

Linking key perspectives in operations due diligence

Linking markets/marketing – products and services

- Scope: does the company have an unduly complex coverage of its markets and its product range – by industry, by channel, by geographic market and by customer segment – making it difficult to gain a strategic focus?

- Fit: do the company's product and services match changing customer needs and lifecycle effects?

- Strategy: is the company's marketing strategy consistent with, and fully supported by, its current and planned products?

Linking markets/marketing with technology

- Market structures: are new technologies likely to reshape the ways in which business is delivered and forms of competition?

- Competitors: are the company's technologies falling behind those of existing competitors and new entrants?
- Futures: is the company's technology capability of sufficient quality to deliver market needs over the forecast time period of cash inflows?

Linking markets/marketing with organization

- Brand: is the company's brand proposition and service delivery consistent with its organizational behaviours, skills and mind-set?
- Mind-set: do company staff exhibit a market-orientated mind-set?
- Change: is the organization sufficiently innovative to deal with rapid market change?

Linking products and services with organization and people

- Resources: does the company have robust enough HR policies and packages to attract and retain key technical skills?
- •Skills: does the company have critical skills gaps in servicing its technical products and services requirements – both now and in the future?

Linking products and services with technology

- Obsolescence: are its current products and services liable to obsolescence due to pending advances in technology?
- Keeping in the game: how much might it cost to develop and support to next-generation products?

Linking technology and organization and people

- Re-engineering: will new technologies allow us to change the organizational structure of the acquisition and enhance its skills to give us a new and lower cost base, and greater flexibility?
- Flexibility: is the present organizational mind-set flexible enough to adapt to new technologies.

Having examined these integrative perspectives, the next step is to look at each perspective individually. This entails a combination of analysis tools and of also asking some key diagnostic questions.

MARKETS / PRODUCTS	1	2	3	4
1				
2				
3				
4				

Figure 5.2 Acquisition target's positioning.

- Products and services
- Technology and IT
- Operations and people
- Manufacturing

SMART QUOTES

Jeremy Clarkson on BMW's integration of Rover

The Germans, they must have gone to a traditional British pub and said 'Ja, the English, they are liking the wood and the leather, so I've put it on the dashboard [of the Rover 75], see the lights of the fruit machine in the corner, we will put these flashing lights on the dashboard, Ja this is very British' – This is like saying that all Germans wear leather shorts and green hats; it is like fitting an onion holder to the dashboard to make it French; it is stupid!

Markets and marketing

To understand our acquisition's markets, the acquisition champion needs to understand its relative competitive strength across the range of its product/markets segments (see Figure 5.2). This can be conveniently evaluated by using a scoring technique as follows:

- Three ticks = very strong

- Two ticks = average strength

- One tick = weak

- No ticks = no presence (in that product market)

Further analysis can be performed by looking at the relative attractiveness of the various product/market segments. This is based on the following major criteria:

- Environmental volatility

- Future growth rate (or 'growth drivers')

- Relative competitive pressure

Again we have for market attractiveness:

- Three ticks = very attractive

- Two ticks = moderately attractive

- One tick = low attractiveness

A further piece of analysis can de performed (where sufficient data are available for business and financial performance). Again we would score:

- Three ticks = strong performance

- Two ticks = average performance

- One tick = weak performance

To illustrate this, look at an overlay of these grids for the Rover Group in 1994 (Figure 5.3). (Here, business and financial performance has been inferred.) This highlights not only the considerable spread of Rover's product/market portfolio but also its dependency upon the Discovery four-wheel drive model. This also helps to highlight the complementary fit with the product/market segments of the acquirer.

Some more detailed criteria for judging market attractiveness are now listed:

Environmental volatility

- Political factors (and regulatory)

MARKETS / PRODUCTS	SMALL-NICHE	VOLUME - SMALL/ MEDIUM	VOLUME - LARGER	NICHE - LARGER	SPORTS	FOUR WHEEL DRIVE	CRITERIA
METRO		✔ ✔ ✔					Attractiveness Strength Performance
MINI	✔ ✔✔✔ ✔✔						Attractiveness Strength Performance
200 & 400		✔ ✔ ✔					Attractiveness Strength Performance
600 & 800			✔ ✔ ✔				Attractiveness Strength Performance
MGF					✔✔✔ ✔✔ ✔✔		Attractiveness Strength Performance
DISCOVERY						✔✔✔ ✔✔✔ ✔✔✔	Attractiveness Strength Performance

Figure 5.3 Rover Group – positioning as at 1994.

- Economic factors

- Social factors

- Technological factors

Growth drivers

- Latent customer needs

- Relative competitive strength of this product relative to substitute products/services

- Ease of consumption by consumers

- Lifecycle effects

- Fashion

- Extent of psychological attractiveness

- Any psychological repulsion to the product

Competitive pressure

- Bargaining power of buyers (from you)

- Bargaining power of supplies (to you)

- The degree of rivalry between companies

- The threat of new entrants

- The threat of substitutes

(Note: do try to think about the future, and not just the present.)

Product/market analysis

For either a past or current acquisition, using Figure 5.3 (along the lines of the Rover Group example):

KILLER
QUESTIONS

- What does this tell you about the relative attractiveness and performance of the acquisition, and also its degree of complexity?

- Does this analysis suggest that you should try to be selective on which parts of the business you buy/don't buy (or rationalize or close down)?

- •Does this analysis change your view of future investment requirements due to the apparent complexity?

- Does it revise your thinking about what it is worth?

Marketing strengths and weaknesses

KILLER
QUESTIONS

- Does the company rely on in-house or external skills for its:
  - Brand strategy?
  - Advertising and promotions?
  - Market research?
  - Other?

- Does the company have a market-led mind-set both at top and senior management level?

- Does the company lead the market and competitive mind-set of the industry, or follow it, or actually lag behind it?

- Does the company's organization demonstrate the capacity to act at a rate which exceeds the rate of market change, or at one which is less than that rate?

Products and services

The detailed appraisal of the target's products and services entails some competitive bench-marking of its strengths and weaknesses by the acquisition champion. To perform competitive bench-marking necessitates some thinking through the use of Kenichi Ohmae's (1982) 'three Cs' framework, of:

• Customer value-added

• Company delivery – of this value (and relative cost)

• Competitor delivery – of this value (and relative cost)

(See Figure 5.4 to understand this three-cornered analysis.)

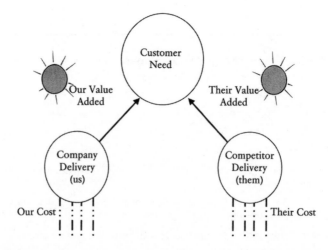

Figure 5.4 Customer–company–competitor analysis. Note: it is essential to take a customer view when looking at value. Also, both value and cost of delivery need comparing.

To understand customer value we need to explore:

- What gets the customer locked-in?

- How relatively important are these factors?

- How well does the company *actually* deliver these?

This comparison may need to be performed separately for different product/market segments, but especially for the 20 per cent of those segments which add 80 per cent of value.

Customer value bench-marking can be done either (i) by asking a sample of real customers, or (ii) by imagining that you are the customer yourself (which you can usually do).

The comparison of relative costs is more difficult because internal data may be harder to come by, especially without unethical espionage. However, where there are good proxies for understanding cost drivers, a reasonable estimate of relative cost is usually feasible. Useful proxies include:

- Relative economies of scale (especially for manufacturing and materials costs)

- Head office and site location (is this de luxe or modest?)

- Salary and wage rates relative to industry norms

- Likely labour productivity, given the quality of the labour force and manufacturing and other processes

- Corporate mind-set (is this relaxed or stringent on costs)

- Attitudes to financial control and to commercial management generally

	Very strong	Strong	Average	Weak	Very weak
	5	4	3	2	1
Brand image					
Product performance					
Service quality					
Innovation drive					
Cost base					
Supporting systems					
Support skills					

Figure 5.5 *Competitor profiling.*

Competitor profiling is a helpful way of displaying competitor position-ing. Figure 5.5 gives a useful format for comparing two different companies. (These criteria can – and should – be changed to fit the par-ticular competitive context and industry.)

In using this profile it is important that:

• Some customer and other objective data is used – at least in present-ing the profiles.

• You position your competitor first on the grid (and not yourself) – to avoid bias.

• The criteria (left-hand side) are both complete and tailored to the industry.

- No more than two companies must be shown on the profile simultaneously (otherwise it seems complex and confusing).

Had Rover been positioned on the grid as at 1994 it would have emerged as being strategically weak and highly vulnerable – the four-wheel drive division excluded.

Techco case

Some yeas ago a strategy consultancy was asked to investigate the division of a technology company, Techco plc, to examine whether it was worth acquiring. The consultancy team interviewed a number of customers, to draw up a profile of its competitive strengths and weaknesses. While the company was still mainly young and thrusting, it suffered from some significant competitive weaknesses.

In particular, the aggressive cut and thrust of its sales force was disliked, especially by its more traditional customers, particularly in the public sector. One customer in a telephone interview, was quoted as saying:

'Oh I know Techco, whenever they do a sales presentation with our senior management it is like being in a Wild West movie. They just act like hired guns whose sole task is to get your order before they are onto the next town.'

Curiously one of the consultants who was on the acquisition investigation team subsequently left the consulting company. A few years later – in another consultancy role elsewhere – he happened to work for Techco management team to develop its strategy. To his amazement, the company's impressive looking sales office actually had pictures of cowboys on the wall – which caricatured their leading sales people – echoing the earlier customer bench-marking.

The Techco case example is quite extraordinary in how accurate customer bench-marking and competitor profiles can be. In fact Techco was bought by a different plc, which we might call Neptulia plc, with a very traditional culture.

Neptulia had been in the engineering industry previously and – like

Nokia – had stumbled into telecommunications. But they never understood Techco's culture. Indeed it was once said at Techco's before a visit by senior management from group HQ:

> The managers from the Planet Neptulia are coming – we had better leave our fleet of Mercedes around the back so they do not get the wrong impression.

(Neptulia plc had a much inferior car scheme.) Needless to say the marriage of Neptulia plc and Techco did not work out. Techo subsequently incurred major losses after its products became out of date technologically – due to under-investment and new entrants. It was then sold off again, then partially turned around and then went into a second phase of major losses and restructuring.

KILLER
QUESTIONS

Products and services due diligence
- For each major product line, what does a competitor profile suggest about its
  - current competitive positioning and gaps between its position and key competitors?
  - future investment needs?
- How complex is the product range and does this produce unduly high operational costs and reduced organizational flexibility and responsiveness?
- How effective are after-sales services and how do these compare with the competition?
- What is the current and potential future cost of regulatory compliance?
- Are there any potential risks of future claims for defective or damaging products?

Technology

Technology capability is another critical area of operations due diligence. Technology may underpin the target's competitive advantage in a number of ways:

- Brand advantage: what is its contribution to a 'high-tech' image? These advantages can still be beneficial long after any advantages from being the first to do something new have expired.

- Product superiority: hard-to-imitate advantages inherent in the product (whether patented or not).

- Customer lock-in: IT systems which make it ultra-convenient and cheap for the customer to deal with the company rather than others.

- Service delivery: using technology to minimize customer's lifecycle of costs.

- Transaction processing: highly cost effective use of IT.

- Customer intelligence/marketing: clever customer databases which can secure additional sales.

A company's technology is embedded in its physical products, in its processes and is manifest too in the thoughts and behaviour of its staff. Technology due diligence thus requires an appraisal of all these manifestations – to identify not just 'what has our target got?' in the way of technological edge, but also 'how effectively is it using it?'

Finally IT systems will require due diligence in their own right. Consider the following key questions:

- How flexible are these systems – for further development?

KILLER
QUESTIONS

Strategic due diligence of technology

- How sustainable is the existing technology base? (That is what might we need to do/or spend to keep up with external changes and even to anticipate that change?)
- How effectively is it being used?
- Is the technology emphasis appropriate, given shifts in the external markets and in changing forms of competition?
- Is it actually sufficient to achieve the strategic goals we would like to set for the acquisition, post-integration, especially in terms of:
  - New customer capture?
  - Volume of business, and transactions?
  - Channel penetration?
  - Speed to market?
  - Increasing service standards?
  - Unit cost reduction?
- How dependent is the company on specific technology skills (perhaps in a small group of key individuals)? Also, how vulnerable is it to losing them either in the period just before or after completion date especially to competitors seizing the chance to poach them?

- How genuinely integrated are IT systems?

- Are there adequate back-up/disaster planning arrangements in place?

- How genuinely 'paper free' are office processes?

- Is the company over-dependent upon external software suppliers/consultants?

- What is the quality of telecommunications systems, e.g. call centres?

- How high/low are IT costs (relative to sales/industry norms)?

Tactical questions for technology due diligence

- What are the company's key technologies?
- How important are these in adding value:
  - defensively?
  - offensively?
- Does the company own these technologies?
- Where it does own the technologies, when are key patents due to expire?
- How strong are these patents?
- Where the company gets its technology from outside (e.g. via an alliance/licensing arrangement), what are the terms of this arrangement and what might their impact be?
- What key technologies do key competitors have but the target either does not have, or is weak in?
- To what extent are the company's key technological processes well documented, and thus might knowledge be potentially lost if many staff leave?
- How up-to-date are these processes?
- Does the company genuinely have a technology strategy which spells out the key areas for technology exploitation and development and how much this is likely to cost over the next 2–3 years? If not, how significant is this gap?

- How IT fluent are staff (including senior management)?

- Does the company genuinely have an IT strategy and one that can develop the business strategy over the next three years?

The following and continuing case on BMW and Rover illustrates and underlines the importance of technology due diligence.

BMW's acquisition of Rover – technology dependency on alliances

Alliance 1 – Honda

When BMW acquired Rover it knew that Rover was tied into a longer-term technology transfer alliance with Honda. Honda supplied the platform technology for the Rover 600 and for other models. Not only did this preclude Rover selling its 600 model in the US, but also this pushed up Rover's unit costs.

Expert industry commentators at the time described Rover as 'Honda's most profitable overseas operation', and the alliance agreement as 'the Honda bear-hug'.

Put simply, Honda was able to exercise its immense bargaining power in a securing a highly favourable arrangement through this alliance. Our verdict: Rover was hugely technologically dependent and weak in this area.

Alliance 2 – Unipart

Also, Rover was dependent on Unipart plc for its parts operation, and upon Unipart's logistics systems. Again industry commentary suggests that BMW was not as aware as it might have been of this dependency, which was crucial in supporting not only the UK business but also its exports. As one source put it: 'BMW seemed to assume that Rover had its own parts department – but that was actually Unipart. So it then had to try to buy Unipart in order to support Rover's overseas drive – for around £150 million.'

Operations and people

The due diligence of organization and people is one of the most important areas for scrutiny by the acquisition champion. While we have already touched on some of the skills areas – and organizational mind-set – in earlier questions there are a number of more detailed areas to probe.

But before moving on to look at the detailed considerations that an acquirer will need to make about an organization and people, let us return to the case of BMW and Rover Group.

What do you get when you try to get a pig to sing – two things. One, the pig can't do it. Two, you even annoy the pig.

M. Hammer and J. Champy, *Re-engineering the Corporation*

Organization and people – at BMW and Rover Group

BMW expected to find a relatively strong management team in place at Rover Group. This led them to believe that a more hands-off integration strategy vis-à-vis organization and people change was appropriate. Unfortunately these assumptions turned out to be misplaced.

This had a number of significant implications:

1. BMW had to replace a number of Rover's top management team. This was implemented after delay – only beyond 18 months following the acquisition – which slowed Rover's integration considerably.

2. BMW managers spent considerable amounts of time to help develop Rover Group's brand strategy. Arguably, Rover's skills in this area were not up to the task ahead.

3. Both the loss of technology input from Honda and the need to fundamentally upgrade Rover's product strategy meant that BMW had to support Rover's redesign effort to an unexpected degree. This entailed a considerable number of BMW's R&D staff being seconded to the UK. This was said to have kept the airlines very busy (and at one point BMW actually chartered a plane for a shuttle service to the UK).

These gaps were not only expensive to address but also carried with them a significant opportunity cost. How many new BMW models could have been designed using this scarce resource and investment – over the period 1995–1999, had BMW not acquired Rover? Would BMW's investment in Rover of around £3 billion over this period have paid for:

- A BMW 2 series?
- A new range of exclusive, world-class sports cars?
- A 'people mover' and a four-wheel-drive series?

See now some of the killer questions that you now need to ask in order to perform adequate due diligence in the areas of organization and people (see opposite page).

Misalignment of organization and people with that of the acquired company (especially during the integration phase) is one of the main reasons why acquisitions fail – and especially for destroying 'V3': the value added during integration.

It is imperative that this aspect of due diligence is handled with care, with rigour, and yet with sensitivity.

In addition to the core areas of operations due diligence (access all companies), there are also more specific data requirements for manufacturing operations. The following questions should now be asked:

Manufacturing facilities

- What are the principle items of machinery and equipment?

- How up to date are these?

- How do these compare against competitors' facilities?

- What condition are these in?

- What degree of utilization do these facilities have?

- What is their replacement cost, their net book value, and what depreciation rates have been used?

- In the future, do these manufacturing assets provide a basis for sustainable competitive advantage?

Organization and people due diligence

KILLER QUESTIONS

- What are the bases of directors' service contracts?
- What are the main conditions of employment for employees generally?
- What are the current pensions arrangements for management and staff, and are company pension schemes fully funded?
- Are CVs available for key staff?
- Is an organization chart available and is this up to date?
- Are there descriptions of key roles and responsibilities?
- What holiday arrangements exist?
- Who is potentially eligible for bonuses, and on what basis?
- Are there any reviews of organization competencies and what gaps/strengths do these highlight?
- What training programmes are in place?
- Have high-potential managers been identified, and what experience do they have?
- What is the age profile, and profile of service length throughout the organization?
- Which staff is it worthwhile interviewing to ask about the company's future?
- What are the company's core values – what kind of culture does it have, and how might this impact on acquisition integration?
- Do any key staff show a reluctance to change?
- How does the company actually value staff and treat them?
- What key HR processes are in place, especially for:
  - recruitment?
  - performance management?
  - development reviews?
  - discipline and dismissal?
  - succession planning?

- organization development, team-building and change management?
- industrial relations?

• Does the company have an HR strategy and what does this strategy tell you? (And not tell you, i.e. what are the gaps?)

• For each of the above bullet points:
  - What are the key differences between target's processes and provisions and your own?
  - What are the costs and benefits of harnessing these?
  - What are the costs and risks of not harnessing these?

Manufacturing processes

• What are the key manufacturing processes, and how advanced are these technologically?

• Are there methods of ensuring zero defect?

• Do these rely on 'just-in-time' production?

• How standardized are procedures?

• How reliable are subcontractors?

• Are cycle times competitive?

Purchasing

• To what extent is the company prone to industry shortages?

• How competitively are supplies being sourced and are suppliers financially strong?

- How does the company monitor and control the quality of purchases?

- Are purchasing procedures robust enough in terms of internal control?

Summary

The process of due diligence naturally follows on from the higher-level evaluation of the acquisition's overall strategy, especially in the areas of markets and marketing, products and services, and in technology. During due diligence we need to conduct a more refined analysis of the target's position in its different product/market segments, and against specific competitors.

The underlying technology base is important too: without a technology edge the target's competitive advantage and financial performance may soon be eroded.

Organization and people issues can be of decisive influence in determining eventual success – especially as this is the area where there is perhaps most potential for value destruction (through 'V3' the value added during integration).

Besides evaluating the acquisition by these separate perspectives it is also essential to look at the interrelationships between perspectives, to avoid looking at each area of due diligence in relative isolation.

6

Financial Evaluation

Championing the business case

The acquisition project leader needs to take a major role in championing the business case. This entails having a good knowledge of its economic fundamentals, of its strategic assumptions, and of how it will be perceived by its key stakeholders.

In this chapter we show you how to think through – step-by-step – the key issues associated with putting together a business case.

But before we do this, it might be helpful to look at what might be a good format for a business case.

We have already seen one crude approach to understanding the value of an acquisition using the V1–V2–V3 typology, where:

- V1 is the value inherent in the business strategy itself.

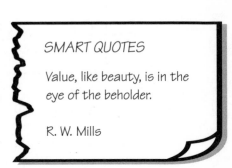

SMART QUOTES

Value, like beauty, is in the eye of the beholder.

R. W. Mills

SMART
BUSINESS
CASE

- Acquisition goals
  - strategic
  - financial
  - operational
  - organizational
- Acquisition options – organic, acquisitive and alliance
- Attractiveness of options – the Strategic Option Grid (and of opportunities foreclosed)
- Detailed competitive assessment
  - strengths and weaknesses
  - external changes and impact
- Integration strategy
  - marketing
  - operations
  - technology and IT
  - organization
- Financial evaluation
  - acquisition scenarios
  - financial projections
  - returns (not present value, impact on earnings per share)
- Assumptions
  - risk assessment
  - risk avoidance planning

- V2 is the value added through the particular deal.

- V3 is the value created or destroyed through post-acquisition management.

We have also seen how V1 can be understood more deeply through the GE grid, appropriately supported by the analysis from Chapter 5. More specifically a number of techniques from that chapter help to provide better support for understanding current and future value generation, especially:

- The five competitive forces – this helps to understand the robustness of margins, and also to identify shifts in the industry structure, for example through new competitor's entering the market or through changes in distribution channel strategy.

- The growth drivers – for understanding the sustainability of expansion in the market or in the companies turnover.

- Target's competitive position: a weak position (like that of Rover in 1994) might entail considerable future investment.

But there are very many ways of understanding value which can be obtained by segmenting it in new ways. For example, consider the following segmentation of value into the future: enhancing and protective value, future opportunity value, synergistic value and sweat value:

- *Enhancing and protective value.* This is the value that can be added either by strengthening the acquired business's *current* competitive position and scope; and the value to the acquirer of a defensive nature, for instance, in avoiding the loss of economies of scale.

- *Opportunity value.* This is the value of the opportunity stream inherent in both the acquired company's markets and its existing platform. This value can come from possible new products, services, network channels or technologies, or simply through fast market growth generally.

- *Synergistic value.* This is the value of bringing together particular activities within the business value systems.

- *Sweat value.* This is the value released by pure reduction of costs or assets in the acquired company, or the potential disposal of whole businesses.

Figure 6.1 shows how this value segmentation can be pictured in diagrammatic form. It shows how Lloyds Bank's acquisition of the Cheltenham & Gloucester Building Society in the UK appeared (based

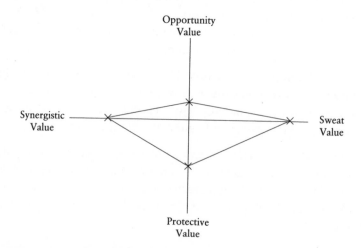

Figure 6.1 Value segmentation.

on press commentary) to be viewed. Figure 6.1 is also useful for under-standing *controlling* and *learning* from acquisitions during integration. Did the assumed synergies prove feasible? Was the opportunity stream (the value) as attractive and as reachable as was originally thought? Did we make the cost base and assets 'sweat' as hard (and as quickly) as we anticipated?

SMART QUOTES

Another approach for the acquisition champion to linking strategy and valuation is to use a pictorial way of representing value through using value and cost drivers.

Here we draw up separate pictures for the major high-level value drivers and also the high-level cost drivers. Figures 6.2 and 6.3 show how this was used to understand BMW's acquisition of Rover more effectively.

Notice on these figures the dependence of Rover Group on the value generation from the four-wheel-drive Discovery model. Also notice the number of major cost drivers reducing the value generation of Rover (Figure 6.3).

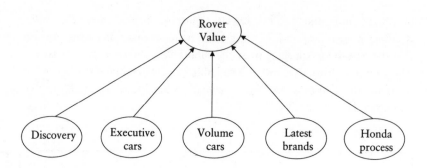

Figure 6.2 Rover's value drivers.

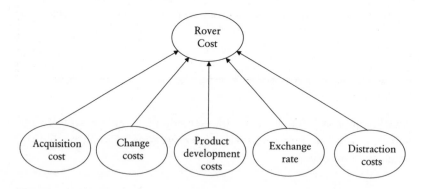

Figure 6.3 Rovers's cost drivers.

Where one company acquires or merges with another one, it is possible actually to assess the shareholder value created or destroyed. This can be put simply as follows:

The added value from the acquisition	=	The value of the acquirer and the acquired's combined shares after the acquisition, less their aggregate value beforehand

This equals the value of acquirer and the acquired's cash streams before the acquisition, plus or minus any positive or negative synergies post acquisition, minus any transaction costs.

So now that you have thought deeper about the kinds of value that an acquisition might generate, and have looked briefly at the impact on share price; let us now look at the bases of valuation and their pros and cons.

Bases of valuation: earnings, assets, discounted cash flows

For the acquisition champion the main ways of valuating a business are:

- The price–earnings ratio
- Assets-based valuation
- Discounted cash flow

The price–earnings ratio is a standard ratio based on industry norms of company value to accounting profits. These accounting profits are likely to be adjusted to reflect necessary changes required (either real, or simply due to changed accounting practices) which will impact on accounting profit. The adjusted accounting profit figure is then called the 'sustainable earnings'.

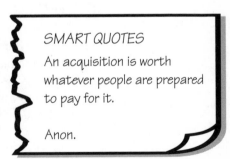

SMART QUOTES

An acquisition is worth whatever people are prepared to pay for it.

Anon.

The assets-backing method looks at the net assets of the company. This figure gives a 'fall-back' valuation (albeit approximate) of what the company might be worth in a forced sale or in a break-up situation. (But do be warned that should this ever happen, then the acquisition value could turn out to be significantly less.)

The discounted cash flow approach calculates the present value of future net cash flows of the acquisition.

The relative pros and cons of these three approaches are as shown in Table 6.1

In sum, the discounted cash flow method is superior on technical grounds to both the price–earnings ratio and to net-assets. Nevertheless, it would be most unusual not to calculate a price–earnings ratio, even if only as a benchmark. Even today the price–earnings ratio is often used at the primary yardstick for valuing a business.

Price–earnings ratios

Price–earnings ratios are used to value a company on the basis of accounting profits (after tax). For example, if a company's after-tax profits are £4 million and it is valued on the basis of a price–earnings ration of 11.5, its potential value is around £4 millon × 11.5 or £46 million.

This valuation is highly approximate for three main reasons:

Table 6.1

Method	Pros	Cons
Price–earnings ratio	• Is already understood (usually) • Can be related to industry benchmarks	• May well inflate the value (unless downsides are factored in) • Ignores the cost of future investment to sustain the business • Is concentrated on the past rather than future
Net assets	• Less subjective than applying a price–earnings ratio	• May not be recouped if the acquisition is unsuccessful • Asset values are subjective – especially if based on replacement
Discounted cash flow	• Is based on a theoretically robust method • Takes into account the full investment to sustain net cash flows	• Some managers, accountants still find it hard to understand • Can be easily manipulated – introducing bias, the terminal value (i.e. the lumpsum value of the cash stream at the end of the forecast time period). May be optimistic

1. 'Earnings' need to be adjusted to be placed on a 'sustainable earnings' basis. This requires a number of adjustments to be made, some of which may not be completely free from subjectivity and may depend on assumptions.

2. The appropriateness of accounting-based earnings can be questioned –these are only indirectly related to cash-flow potential, and the data are essentially historic, and might provide a misleading guide to the future.

3. The price–earnings ratio itself needs to be benchmarked, which may not be particularly easy where the company might be in an unusual sector.

Accounting profits might be misleading due to:

Smart things to say about financial valuation

Don't panic, take it one step a time!

• Accounting adjustments for non-cash items (like depreciation and provisions) can produce a quite different basis from valuation based on sustainable net cash flow.

• In a situation of rapid development and competitive change, future investment requirements may well significantly exceed past levels.

Supposing we have the following basic figures:

Target's profit and loss account

	£million
Turnover	200
Cost of sales	130
Gross profit	70
General and administrative expenses	36
Operating profit	34
Interest payable	10
Corporation tax	8
Profit for ordinary shareholders	16

The unadjusted valuation using a price–earnings ratio of 10 is therefore £16 million × 10 or £160 million.

In this illustration the acquirer plans to rationalize the head office of target, saving £4 million a year. Also, to align target's accounting practices for depreciation with those of the new group will cost £2 million a year. In addition, £2 million of recent earnings has been due to an alliance, which has now expired.

This means that sustainable earnings are now as follows:

	£million
Previous operating profit before interest	34
Add back head office cost reduction	4
Less depreciation	(2)
Less alliance contract now expired	(4)
Adjusted earnings before tax and interest	32
Less interest payable	10
Less corporation tax	7.4
Sustainable profit for ordinary shareholders	14.6

The adjusted value using a price–earnings ratio of 10 is therefore £14.6 million × 10 or £146 million.

This valuation of £146 million is the *value to the acquirer*, and not be the appropriate offer price. The offer price might well be based on the above adjusted figures (after taking out the extra depreciation and the revenue from the alliance contract), but *not* after adjusting for the reduction in head office costs. (One should argue that the £2 million assumed head office cost savings are what the acquirer brings to the party, and should not be shared with the vendor.)

A 'full' price, i.e. the maximum price one might ever consider paying, would (on this basis) look like:

	£million
Operating profit	34
Less additional depreciation	(2)
Less alliance contract now expired	(4)
Adjusted earnings before tax and interest	28
Less interest payable	(10)
Less corporation tax	(6)
Sustainable profit for ordinary shareholders	12

The full price for this acquisition at a price–earnings ratio of 10 would be £12 million × 10, or £120 million.

The range of values for the acquisition target, even though calculated on a similar basis, thus turned out to be quite different.

Chapter 7, 'Managing the Deal', goes into the dynamics of the deal in more depth.

An important thing to note here that if we were to take the vendor's perspective here, one might well argue that the head office cost savings were only possible *if the vendor was prepared to actually sell this business.* In that context, the vendor could (perhaps plausibly) argue that some of the value of these cost savings thus belongs to the vendor, and not to the acquirer. A strong vendor will then wish to share in the value created by the deal. The way to make this value-sharing a reality in practice is simply to threaten competitive bidding for the acquisition.

It is always essential you as acquisition champion define a 'walk-away from' price: this is the price at which the acquirer will threaten to pull out of the deal (and actually carry that threat out, if need be).

The walk-away from price needs to provide sufficient leeway and contingency allowance for things not working out in a completely ideal world. So, taking our above example once again, we have:

1. Unadjusted valuation   £160 million

2. Adjusted valuation   £146 million

3. Full price   £120 million

4. Contingency for things going wrong 10%   £12 million

5. Walk-away from price   £108 million (3 – 4)

The price–earnings ratio above estimates the post-acquisition earnings

---

The 'walk-away from' price

You can adjust the valuation, based on latest data relative to a bench-mark. There is much less likelihood of getting carried away.

Smart things
to know

for the target for a single period, and assumes that this level will be maintained. There is therefore no recognition in a simple price-earnings ratio of the future pattern of earnings growth. For example, operating profit margin or sales volumes (or both) might increase significantly.

There are also significant problems in defining the most appropriate bench-mark for earnings. Whilst there may be similar companies to compare with, the quality of past earnings, and their exposure to market areas which on either inherently likely to expand or contract will be different.

The model also does not explicitly consider the investor-perceived risk of the target firm's earnings which may have high, medium or low volatility.

When buying an unquoted company there may be no objective yardstick to apply. One might apply a broad-brush discount of 25–30% off an equivalent publically-traded company (perhaps an even greater discount) – to reflect the greater difficulty of disposing of shares, but this is highly approximate in deriving a benchmark price–earnings ratio.

Assets backing

A primitive view of the worth of an acquisition is the historic value of its net assets. A net assets valuation at least gives us some kind of fall-back position – if trading deteriorates – even though it gives us no indication whatsoever of a company's future earnings potential. But unfortunately, many assets on the balance sheet may not be worth their written-down historic value upon a forced sale or closure. Whilst debtors ought to be realized more or less in full, the value of written-down fixed assets may

For an acquisition that you have either bought in the past or are currently thinking about buying:

- What is/has been the quality of past earnings growth? Consider

  - Year-on-year earnings fluctuations

  - The impact of exceptional items

  - Vulnerability to market and competitive pressures

- What is the likely quality of future earnings growth?

- How turbulent and uncertain is the industry generally?

- How sensitive is that particular trend of business to pending boom in the economy, or potentially a slow-down or recession?

- Is the sector susceptible to investor fashion (like the dotcom market during 1999–2000), and when is fashion likely to evaporate?

- How does this company compare to other companies in the sector (both quoted and unquoted) – in terms of quality of future prospects?

- Given the above considerations, what appears to be a sensible price–earnings ratio range for this company?

be less than net book value on a quick exit from the business. Stocks might be worth half (or even less) of historic value as any receiver knows. Properties, also might yield disappointing disposal values on a sale under pressure.

Net assets are usually valued (after depreciation) at amounts considerably less than either a price-earnings valuation or a discounted cash flow valuation. One approach to closing this gap is to re-evaluate net assets using replacement costs. This can be useful in spotting undervalued companies. One approach is to calculate:

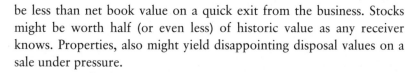

$$\frac{\text{Market value of assets}}{\text{Book value (at replacement costs)}}$$

Where this ratio (known as the "market to book ratio") is less than one, there ought to be (other things being equal) a major opportunity for either selling off the assets, improving profitability (or both).

Example – assets backing of target

Our target's summary balance sheet is as follows:

At historic cost	£million	£million
Fixed assets:		
Properties	30	
Plant and equipment	12	
		42
Intangible assets		14
Current assets:		
Stocks	16	
Debtors	30	
Cash	6	
	52	
Less creditors	(10)	
Less bank loans	(16)	
		26
		82
Long term liabilities:		
Bank loans	12	
Net assets	70	

The following adjustments now need to be made to arrive at replacement values:

1. Property revaluation: from £30 million to £40 million.

2. Plant and equipment: written down from £12 million to £10 million

3. Stocks: written down from £16 million to £14 million (possible obsolescence)

4. Contingent liabilities which might crystallize on sales of £6 million, requiring a provision.

5. Intangible assets need to be written off by £10 million.

Replacement cost balance sheet

Replacement values:	£million	£million
Fixed assets:		
Properties	40	
Plant and equipment	<u>10</u>	
		50
Intangible assets		4
Current assets		
Stocks	14	
Debtor	26	
Cash	<u>6</u>	
	46	
Less creditors	10	
Less bank loans		

		20
		74
Long-term liabilities – loans	12	
Other provisions	6	
		18
Net assets(replacement value)		56

Discounted cash flow

Discounted cash flow (or 'DCF') focuses on the economic cash flow (sometimes called the 'economic profit') which the acquisition's strategy is expected to yield in the future. This 'economic profit' will be different from projected future accounting profits as the latter is drawn up on the accruals concept where revenues are matched against costs for a particular time period making adjustment for depreciation and other non-cash charges. Cash flows are actually therefore a more fundamental basis of financial valuation.

Smart things
to say about discounted
cash flow

Capital is never free –
it has a rental

So how can the acquisition champion begin to get his/her head around the logic of discounting cash flows and of NPV (or 'net present value'). Having cleared away any possible confusion between accounting and economic profit.

The detailed procedure for discounting

Discounting future cash flows involves reducing the value future cash flows to reflect the fact that cash at some future date is worth less than cash held at present. This is just the same as investing in a building society with the expectation that at some future date you will receive *more* money back in the way of principle plus interest, for instance at an interest rate of 10%. Discounting is, in effect, the same procedure in reverse – the investor would be indifferent between having, for instance, £121 after two years and £100 now, or:

$$\frac{£121}{(1.10) \times (1.10)} = £100$$

where 1.10 is equivalent to 100 plus 10%.

In discounted cash flow we apply a *discount factor*, whether this is from a discount table or a spreadsheet package. At the end of year 2 this factor is, one divided by (1.10 times 1.10) is 0.826. One might be inclined to ask here 'what does this factor of 0.826 mean?' What this means is, given the attitude of the investor to holding money now versus the future, in order to get an equivalent valuation of a cash stream occurring over a period in time he needs to adjust for these (time) preferences.

But the end product of this calculation – the 'present value' – has a 'notional' or 'unreal' feel to it, as the business will never receive in hard cash terms the exact value of the 'present value'. The 'present value' is a mixture of cash flows evaluation using successively harsher discount factors at different points in time.

It is possible to revisit a business case by comparing the estimated versus the realized cash flows. The net difference can then be re-evaluated by discounting the difference between estimated and realized cash flows.

It is easy for managers to fall into a number of other

A smart way to get to sleep

Memorize discounted cash flow tables

traps in understanding and applying discounting techniques, especially in the following areas:

- Getting confused between the discount rate and, for instance, the rate of return required to compensate for inflation (the discount rate compensates investors for inflation *plus* a real reward for deferring cash into the future *plus* a further premium for risk on that kind of business investment).

- Projecting cash flows in terms which *do not* incorporate expectations of inflation, and then applying an *inflation-included* discount rate to find a present value. The result is then a present value of future cash flows which is artificially low. The rate applied needs to be consistent at all times.

Also the consequences of applying discounting procedures include, first, that cash inflows later on are, in effect, penalized in the valuation relative to the present value of initial outlays and earlier cash inflows. The higher the discount rate, the more pronounced this penalizing and compounding effect will become. This lowers the value of the investment (its net present value, or 'NPV'). At ten years into the future, a 10% discount rate for example gives a discount factor of approximately 0.38, while a 15% discount rate gives a factor of only 0.25.

Further, the assumed 'terminal value' of the investment in the acquisition can play a major role in determining NPV unless it is (a) included a very long way out into the future; (b) the investment's capital value is much reduced at the end of its lifecycle; (c) the discount rate is very high or (d) a mixture of (a), (b) and (c) occurs. This means that it is easy to manipulate NPV by forming optimistic assumptions for terminal value – a point many readers will no doubt recognize. For example, in one acquisition example the NPV of the deal doubled if the 'terminal value' was evaluated on a price earning ratio of 15 as opposed to 10.

DCF is now applied in the following way:

1. The future cash flows of the target based on the assumptions for its post-acquisition management by the bidder over the forecast horizon is estimated.

2. The terminal value of the target at forecast horizon is assessed.

3. The cost of capital appropriate for the target, given its projected post-acquisition risk and capital structure is assessed.

4. The estimated cash flows is discounted at the cost of capital to give a value of the target.

5. Other cash inflows from sources such as asset disposals or business divestments are added in at present values.

6. Debt and other expenses, such as tax on gains from disposals and divestments, and acquisitions costs are subtracted to give a value from the equity of the target.

7. The estimated value of the equity for the target is then compared with its pre-acquisition stand-alone value to determine the added value from the acquisition.

8. The extent of added value which should be shared with target shareholders as a premium – (without going above one's walk-away from price) should be considered.

In order to get a better grip on the realities underlying *future* net cash inflows the acquisition champion needs to examine the underlying value and cost drivers of a business.

Again conventional thinking often defines value drivers and cash drivers in terms which are very close to quantitative terms. For example, Rappaport (1986) identifies five key value drivers as:

- Forecast sales growth in volume and revenue terms.

- Operating profit margin.

- New fixed capital investment.

- New working capital investment.

- The cost of capital.

Most post-acquisition activity aims at altering the top four above drivers, so that additional value can be created. These value divers are often interdependent. For example, higher sales growth may be achieved only be increasing expenditure on marketing, advertising or product development, or by additional investment in the business – these value drivers then translated provide the assumptions which drive forecast of cash outflows and inflows.

SMART QUOTES

Since acquirers pay a premium for the business, they actually have two business problems to solve: (1) to meet the performance targets the market already expects, and (2) to meet the even higher target's implied by the acquisition premium. This situation is analogous to emerging technology investments where investors pay for breakthroughs that have not yet occurred, knowing that competitors are chasing the same breakthroughs. However, in acquisitions, the breakthroughs are called 'synergies'.

M.L. Sirower, *The Synergy Trap*

The most important value drivers often turned out to be not the above, relatively superficial 'value drivers' but a different and more specific set of drivers. For example, were Tesco to have consummated its contemplated acquisition of Marks and Spencer around 2000, it would have needed to have considered:

- M&S brand strength.

- Changes in consumer tastes – towards branded goods.

- Consumer affluence levels.

- Demographic changes – the 'grey market' (40–55 year olds) wanted to become more fashionable.

- Competitor entry and imitation.

- Commentary from the national press.

And so on . . .

A 'value driver' is defined as *any variable, (either inside or outside of the business) which might help (directly or indirectly) to generate cash inflows.*

Conversely, a cost driver is defined as *any variable (either inside or outside of the business) which might result (directly or indirectly) to cause cash outflows.*

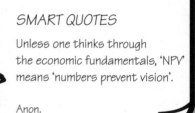

At a more technical level, operating cash inflow are calculated after (corporation) tax cash flows, but before any payment of interest on any borrowing to finance the target. Cash outflows are due to, additional fixed capital and working capital investments. After-tax operating cash flows (which are arrived at after adding back any depreciation previously charged – as this is non-cash) after any investment cash outflows are called 'free cash flows'.

Cash flows are generally forecast for the next five to ten years. Whatever the forecast horizon, the terminal value of the target at the end of that period based on free cash flows also needs to be forecast often this terminal value is based on the assumption of perpetual free cash flows based on the same level of operations as in the last year of the forecast period. These perpetual cash flows (i.e. ones that are assumed to go on for ever) are then capitalized at the cost of capital to calculate the terminal value (see an example coming soon – for an illustration of this).

The forecast free cash-flows provides the acquirer with the value of the target as a whole. From this value, debt is subtracted to give the assumed equity value.

The cost of capital which should be used is called weighted average cost of capital (or WACC). This is estimated from your company's pre-acquisition costs of equity and debt.

We are now entering slightly more technical territory for the acquisition champion – who may not be well schooled in corporate finance. What follows therefore is a gentle introduction.

The following table illustrates a calculation of a target's equity using forecast free cash flows. This is based on the assumptions of:

• Sales growth at 5% per annum between year 1 and 5

• Operating profit margin at 3% following price rises and or cash reduction, rising to 4% of sales post-acquisition

• Additional fixed capital and working capital runs at 10% of incremental sales

• The cost of capital (WACC) calculated as below is 12%

The weighted average cost of capital =

$$\text{cost of capital} \times \frac{\text{market value of capital}}{\text{market value of equity and debt}}$$

$$+\text{cost of debt} \times \frac{\text{market value of debt}}{\text{market value of equity and debt}} \times \left(1 - \text{corporate rate tax}\right)$$

This is just the same as deciding to borrow for a car costing £10,000, with £5,000 from the bank at 15% and £5,000 from a rich uncle at 5%.

The WACC here would be:

$$\frac{15\% \times 5,000}{10,000} + \frac{5\% \times 5,000}{10,000} = £10,000$$

The value of the acquisition's free cash flows is now calculated as:

$$\text{target's value} = \frac{\text{sum of free cash flows for the period}}{(1 + \text{WACC})} + \frac{\text{terminal value}}{(1 + \text{WACC})}$$

This formulae splits into two the valuations of forecast cash flows and the assumed valued cash flows into perpetuity thereafter.

The above formulae assumes that free cash flows during the period after the forecast line horizon are sustainable. (This may not be the case). They also assume that there is no major, lumpy investment required just after the forecast time horizon to reposition or restructure the acquisition. This may be a valid assumption, or it may not be. Also, it is

- What is the proportion of the present value tied up in the terminal value?
- What scenarios have been explored to underpin the terminal value?

Smart questions to ask

assumed that shareholders will not regard the merged companies as more volatile and higher risk. Again, this may not be a valid assumption.

The last thing we need to define is the 'terminal value' which is:

$$\frac{\text{net operating profit less taxes}}{\text{weighted average cost of capital}}$$

(See Copeland *et al.*, 1990.)

DCF analysis of target (in millions of £)

	Base year Year 0	Year 1	Year 2	Year 3	Year 4	Year 5
Sales	100.0	105.0	110.25	115.76	121.54	127.60
Operating profit	3.00	4.20	4.41	4.63	4.86	5.10
Corporation tax	0.99	1.38	1.45	1.53	1.60	1.68
Incremental fixed assets and working capital	–	0.5	0.52	0.55	0.57	0.60
Free cash flows	2.01	2.32	2.44	2.55	2.69	2.82
Discounted at 1/(1+12%) compounded	–	2.07	1.94	1.81	1.71	1.60

So present value of forecast cash flows	=	£9.13 million (A)
Plus terminal value (as at end of Year 5)	=	2.82
Divided by the rest of capital		12%
	=	£23.5 million (B)
Giving a present value of 23.5	=	£13.3 million
		(1+12%) to the power of 5

Which discounts the value of these terminal cash flows to the present.

Total acquisition value is thus £9.13 million plus £13.3 million, or £22.43 million. This means that nearly 60% of target's value is bound up in the present value of its terminal value, which is beyond the period of detailed forecasts. This is not an unusual percentage.

If you are not very familiar with these types of technique go back through these details again, imagining perhaps that you are considering buying a 'buy-to-rent' property. The principles would be identical.

The above example highlights a number of key points:

- The 'terminal value' should not be accepted uncritically, but needs to be supported by, and tested by some story-telling (or more formally, 'scenario development') of the future. This might extend to for example:

  - future growth drivers

  - future competitive conditions

  - future business models and sources of competitive advantage

- The value of the acquisition is very much determined by the terminal value. This value is for a period which we cannot forecast with much reliability, underlining the fact that acquisition values are very much an act of faith to a considerable extent.

- Projections will be particularly sensitive to shifts in operating profit margin. Which is in turn sensitive to the competitive forces of the industry – and of the target's competitive strength.

- 'Present value' is also sensitive to the amount of future investment required to integrate the acquisition in order to in future (a) protect the business, (b) enhance products or to reduce costs and (c) provide capacity for future growth.

Once we have calculated the potential value of the acquisition using all three methods then the next step is to compare these together.

Scenarios and uncertainty and risk analysis

Risk analysis should be conducted not by standard, pre-set, sensitivity percentages, but by a deeper appreciation of the robustries of key variables – the value and cost drivers (those things which either bring cash into the business, or drive it out). To facilitate this is it useful to draw upon both scenario story-telling (about the future), and upon a technique known as the 'Uncertainty Grid'.

SMART QUOTES

Because the acquisition idea must be 'sold' to many groups, the initial justification may be developed so persuasively that it is difficult to dispute, and as a result bandwagon effect may be created because the groups involved cannot imagine how it could fail. This false sense of security clouds the managers' abilities to realise that changing circumstances can affect their prior assumptions and the acquisition's success.

P.C. Haspeslagh and D.B. Jemison, *Managing Acquisitions*

The Uncertainty Grid is shown in Figure 6.4. Here one looks at the assumptions about the world going right, and then proceeds to rate these in terms of: (a) their degree of importance, and (b) their degree of uncertainty.

Once this is done, one positions each assumption on the grid. Where there are assumptions which lie in the South-East section of the grid this

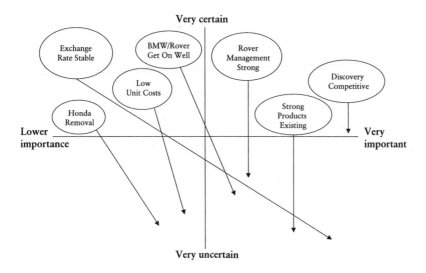

Figure 6.4 Uncertainty–importance grid.

suggests one should do the most robust sensitivity analysis and tolerance testing.

The reason why one frames these assumptions in terms of 'the world going right' (rather than going wrong) is that one can then identify the downsides to the acquisition.

Figure 6.4 uses the methodology for BMW's acquisition of Rover Group. These show BMW's assumptions as follows:

• Rover's unit costs were reasonably low.

• Rover's existing product range (volume cars) was reasonably strong.

- The four-wheel-drive Discovery model would remain highly competitive.

- Rover's depending on Honda could be removed without doubling or trebling existing investment levels.

- Rover's existing management resources were 'strong'.

- BMW would be able to get on well with Rover's management team.

- The UK exchange rate would not strengthen them by over 20%.

becoming *both* more important *and* more uncertain shifting both south and east.

These shifts might have been anticipated before the event – (see Grundy, 1995). The effect of these adverse shifts meant that BMW destroyed shareholder value (according to some sources – see for example, *The Independent*, 28 March 2001) of between £2.5 and £3.0 billion.

Yet at the time the acquisition of Rover (at around £800 million) was felt to be 'cheap'.

SMART QUOTES

Once companies begin intensive integration, the costs of exiting a failing acquisition strategy can become very high. The integration of sales forces, information and control systems, and distribution systems, for example, is often very difficult to reverse in the short term. And in the process, acquirers may run the risk of taking their eyes off competitors or losing their ability to respond to changes in the competitive environment.

M.L. Sirower, The Synergy Trap

But with post acquisition investment in Rover increasing from the £100 million to £150 million per annum level pre-acquisition to around £500 million this acquisition was anything but 'cheap'.

This meant big increases in investment to protect the competitiveness of existing models, and to launch new models – notably the smaller, four-wheel-drive Freelander, the Rover 75, 45 and 25 – and a deluxe mini.

It is fruitful to scope the full investment iceberg of the acquisition (Grundy, 1995). This investment iceberg needs to include:

- Purchase consideration

- Transaction costs

- Restructuring costs – initial

- Restructuring costs – ongoing

- Investment to protect and enhance the existing product range

- Investment in new products – to achieve post-acquisition ambitions and strategy

- The costs of distraction – in terms of scarce management and other time.

Links to the negotiation process

The economic evaluation of an acquisition target is a powerful weapon in the pursuit of a favourable price. A number of tips can assist the acquisition champion considerably in the negotiating process. These include:

- Use the basis for valuation which gives you the most modest price during negotiation (in the example in the previous section this would have been a combination of assets backing and discounted cash flow).

- When using price – income ratios, where the target's past track record has been volatile then this gives you plenty of argument for negotiating a more modest price earnings ratio on the grounds of 'poorer quality of earnings'.

- Where potential contingent liabilities might exist and where the vendor is unwilling to provide sufficient warrantees for these then this provides an argument for reducing the value of the 'assets backing' figure.

- If the company is likely to require increasing investment to sustain its independence – without being acquired – then assume a higher level of future investment when evaluating its free cash flows.

- The present value free cash flows will be reflected by the cost of capital you are using. In theoretical terms there is no real justification for using a premium rate for the cost of capital just because the acquisition is relatively 'risky' – (strictly, this is the 'risk' which should be factored in is that risk which is inherent in that particular type of market or industry). Nevertheless, many parties to the acquisition deal may not appreciate this corporate finance subtlety: so why not just add several percentage-points to your cost of capital to actually allow for this ambiguity?

- As we saw in the example in the previous section, much of the present value of an acquisition is bound up in the terminal value. Instead of assuming that cash flows will continue into perpetuity, one might apply a price-earnings ratio based on an assumed sale of the business. Where the future external market of the target is likely to be more heavily competitive then one might be able to justify a lower price earnings ratio in view of probably declining margins.

- Where one's target is in a number of different businesses (and in effect, industries), then one's price–earnings benchmark might be somewhat flexible. For example where a health-care company had bought a number of private hospitals there might be an argument for using a price-earnings ratio somewhere between that of property company and that of the health industry. (That is of course, where there are a lack of bench-marks for price-earnings ratios of independent private hospitals.)

At the end of the day acquisition valuations can still be shrouded in subjectivity and in agendas. In one acquisition case, for example, the vendor increased the price they wanted from around £15 million to £22 million. The inherent value of the business, based on our three valuation measures was around £12–14 million. After the transaction failed in sheer frustration the Managing Director asked the vendor's merchant banking advisers what their valuation basis has been. They replied, candidly: 'To be completely honest the only basis for that valuation is that you have lots of money, you really need to buy their business, so they wanted to get their hands on that money.'

Summary

The financial evaluation of an acquisition rests as much upon the strategic assumptions as it does upon narrower, operational analysis. This in turn depends upon the underlying assumptions (rather than on the superficial value and cost drivers).

The three main bases of financial evaluation include price–earnings ratios, assets backing, and discounted cash flows. Each basis of valuation needs to be considered and carefully weighed against the underlying assumptions, before arriving at a tentative valuation. This needs testing using story-telling of competitive futures.

The differing bases for valuation can also be used as ammunition within the negotiation process, particularly to set a more realistic tone to discussions of the acquisition's value.

7

Managing the Deal

Introduction: acquisition options and bargaining power

The deal-making process is a critical phase during which the acquisition champion creates 'V2' (see Chapter 1) – this is the value added, diluted or destroyed during the negotiation. In this chapter the role of acquisition options and bargaining power are explored. This is then linked to the deal-making agendas that both parties to the acquisition may have. The role of scenario story-telling for the deal is then explored before a number of tips on 'deal-making do's and don'ts' is elaborated. Finally we look at funding the acquisition, and also at issues surrounding BMW's acquisition of Rover.

Turning first to the role of acquisition options and bargaining power, just which factors will actually determine 'V2'? These can be distilled into five key influences for the acquisition champion to home in on:

• The strength of desire by the acquirer to buy.

• The strength of desire by the vendor to sell.

Particularly in bidding situations, the dynamics of the process, the fact that an acquisition has different values for different bidders, who may overestimate the uncertain benefits because of their desire to win the bid, results in a tendency to bargain away all potential benefits.

P.C. Haspeslagh and D.B. Jemison, *Managing Acquisitions*

- The other options available to the acquirer – either through alternative acquisition, organic development or through alliance.

- The other options available to the vendor – either to dispose of the business to other parties, or to develop or turnaround the business oneself.

- The relative time pressure to do a deal: is it more urgent to the buyer to do a deal, or is it more urgent to the vendor?

Figure 7.1 displays this visually, along similar lines to Porter's Five Competitive Forces (see Porter, 1980).

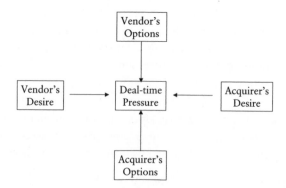

Figure 7.1 Acquisitions: the five forces.

Diagnosing acquisition deal-making processes

KILLER QUESTIONS

The acquirer's desire to buy

- How much perceived growth is there in this particular market?
- How much previous publicity have you given your acquisition strategy (e.g. in your annual report and accounts, press releases and actual deals to date)?
- Who is actually the prime mover on the team, and what is on his/her personal agendas given how long they have been in that role?

The vendor's desire to sell

- Why might the vendor want to sell now?
- Why might the vendor want to sell in the future, given its strategy?
- What is on the personal agendas of the key vendor's representatives who negotiated the deal?

The acquirer's other options

- What options for organic development does the acquirer have?
- What alliance options does the acquirer have?
- What other acquisition options does the acquirer have?
- How attractive and flexible are these options?

The vendor's other options

- What options exist to develop and grow the business organically – without disposal?
- What other options – e.g. to sell to other parties – exist?
- What closure options exist for the vendor (in case of a forced sale)?
- How attractive are these alternative options?

The time-pressure to do a deal

- What specific timetables, deadlines or other corporate pressures are driving the acquirer to want a quick deal?
- What parallel time pressures does the vendor also face?
- Who is under most perceived time pressure – the vendor or the acquirer?

You should now use this model for an acquisition situation which you are currently contemplating.

Understanding deal-making agendas

Figure 7.2 shows how the positions of key stakeholders *vis-à-vis* an acquisition can be represented visually. This gives the acquisition champion a useful map of where the key players will be coming from – and on both sides of the deal. (This technique is an expansion from Figure 4.4 in Chapter 4.)

The merits of this visual approach to understanding agendas (whether this is done very formally – on paper or informally – in one's head) is that:

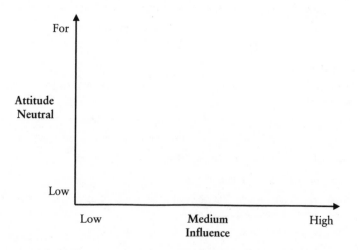

Figure 7.2

- It highlights both the business agendas impacting on key issues and the personal agendas too.

- It helps to identify and deal with political issues by making them more discussible.

- It provides a context for telling scenario stories about how the deal process might go in future, thus helping reduce surprises (see the next subsection below).

- It helps to make the team's powers of observation more acute to get a better feel of where the other side is coming from.

- It also helps to focus influencing strategies and tactics on the really key individuals.

- It can also help the team to reflect itself its own agendas, and to manage its level of commitment to any deal, and to walk away from a deal which has become unattractive.

Having now looked at deal-making agendas, deal scenarios (and associated story-telling) are now explored.

For one acquisition that you are in the process of negotiating, or one you are thinking of doing, or for one that you did in the past:

- What are (were) on the agendas of your team in terms of 'turn-ons' and 'turn-offs', and how relatively strong were those agendas?

- What are (were) on the agendas of the vendor's team, in terms of 'turn-ons' and 'turn-offs', and how relatively strong were those agendas?

- What is the 'so-what'? from this analysis (e.g. in terms of identifying potential negotiating cards on both sides)?

KILLER QUESTIONS

Deal scenarios

Scenario story-telling entails the acquisition champion being able to imagine and anticipate the different moves that you and the vendor are likely to make during the deal. The professional advisers on both sides are also players in the drama. Just as really good chess-players focus around half of their attention on the intent of their competitors (rather than just on their strategy and moves), so in scenario story-telling equal weighting is placed on the vendor's intent.

Using the 'out-of-body experience' and deal-making agendas (which we explained in the last subsection), now put yourself fully within the mind-set, the feelings and the anxieties of the vendor. It may be helpful for one person in your team to actually role-play being the vendor.

It's fruitful to imagine and develop through interactive role-play the agendas of the key players within the vendor's team during:

- The initial contact with the vendor (see also the earlier subsection on 'Approaching the target').

- The first full meeting with the vendor to explore a potential deal.

- The various stages of the due diligence process (where you are likely to discover downsides and drawbacks); here it is useful to imagine especially the interactions that might occur as these downsides are discussed between yourselves and the vendor.

- Possible increases in the acquisition price – due to new, competing bidders for your target emerging.

- Possible reductions in the offer due either to unexpected due diligence issues emerging, or to deliberate tactics on your part to knock the vendor down in a 'forced sale' situation.

- Responses to 'deal stoppers' emerging at a very late stage in negotiations.

- Reactions of the vendor's top management and shareholders to discussions of 'who is going to be doing what' in the new company – especially where these are personally and politically sensitive.

Each of these situations is likely to be complex, uncertain and yet decisive in the outcome of the deal process.

In order to perform scenario story-telling for the dynamics of the deal, it is essential that the acquisition champion is able to be:

- *Creative* – in describing the future context of the story.

- *Fluid* – in linking one event with another (as a chain), and in thinking through the interactions between the various players, and their knock-on effects.

- *Imaginative* – in being able to develop a particular story-line right through to its results and implications.

Example – story-telling of acquisitions at Global Biotechnology plc

A high-technology company, Global Biotechnology plc, was seeking to diversify (through acquisition) into certain biotechnology markets. A small, biotechnology company had been put up for sale by a manufacturing conglomerate that had inadvertently brought its biotechnology business as part of a low-technology and lower-risk set of businesses.

Global Biotechnology had already gained a reputation in the acquisitions market as being extremely keen on making acquisitions within the sector, and also for paying the full price for its acquisitions. Because of previous post-acquisition integration problems, Global Biotechnology decided to field an acquisition team with an impressive skills base with three head office representatives (a corporate planner, a senior tax specialist, and a lawyer) along with four managers of the acquiring division for the first negotiation meeting. The bio-tech acquisition target was small, having a turnover and assets both well under £10 million.

One of the members of the acquisition team was a locum financial director on secondment from the management consultancy of a major accounting firm. It fell to him to tell some scenario stories of how the balance of negotiating power would pan out during the deal.

He knew that the enlarged acquisition team was to meet the opposition in a hotel near to Charles De Gaulle Airport, Paris. So this is how his scenario story-telling went:

'Given that we have fielded a large, prestigious team within Global Biotechnology, this will no doubt signal to the vendor's negotiators that we are very easy prey – and are willing to pay a very full price. In the negotiating process I can foresee that our divisional Managing Director will display undue enthusiasm for conducting a deal, and that once we get two-thirds of the way through the process the vendor's professional negotiators will start to change the goalposts and try to squeeze a significantly better deal than that discussed at the start.

Also, even though we have signed an exclusive negotiating arrangement (for the next six weeks) the vendor will hint that the price which we proposed is simply unrealistic, and that they will need to hang onto crucial parts of the business unless they get a higher price, or otherwise they will simply wait until the six weeks have expired. In the meantime, they will have been contacted by at least two of Global Biotechnology's competitors, who are also desperately keen to enter the industry. The vendor's chief negotiator will not tell us this openly but will simply allude to this possibility. Instead of our team then responding as a unified approach, our common front will disintegrate rapidly with our Chief Executive displaying his obvious impatience with his professional advisers for holding things up.

While we are then ironing out some of the legal technicalities of the deal, some potential deal-stoppers will emerge at the last possible minute – limiting the warrantees and indemnities relative to what we expected and assumed. Although these problems are then partially ironed-out, we are nevertheless led to make concessions that we had not wanted to make at the outset.'

The above scenario was actually not very far from what actually happened. Very quickly the obvious psychological advantage of the vendor's team came to the fore, and any chance at achieving a reasonably balanced deal fell quickly by the wayside.

Postscript to the case: five years later the management consultant actually met one of the vendor's former advisers at a Christmas party. They began reflecting on the acquisition and the former vendor's adviser reflected on it:

'I do remember that Global Biotechnology acquisition. We really managed to take you to the cleaners. We had expected a much, much tougher deal. In fact as I was travelling myself to Paris I actually saw the team attempting to negotiate with a taxi to take them three miles to the hotel – and failing. Such a top-heavy team just did not seem to be able to get its act together, and we were able to pick you off with ease once your Divisional CEO showed overly that he wanted to do a deal at almost any price.'

KILLER
QUESTIONS

Scenarios

For one phase of an acquisition deal that you are either currently working through or are contemplating:

- What scenario stories can you tell about the future dynamics of the deal – given your best understanding of all parties' agendas?

- How will their potential negotiating moves impact on your tactics, and vice versa?

- What deal-stoppers (specifically) are likely to materialize at the last possible moment, and how will you handle these?

- •What cards do you wish to hold back during negotiations in order to maximize your deal-making flexibility, and to gain advantage?

- Who in your team would cause problems of disunity and how can you head these off?

Note: unless you are actually *telling stories* about the future – just as was illustrated in the Global Biotechnology plc case, then you are not genuinely developing scenarios for the deal process.

Recipes for the deal-making process

Deal making do's

A fruitful way for the acquisition champion to manage the negotiation process more effectively is to ponder the following deal-making do's and don'ts: these do's and don'ts have been compiled with the help of the distilled experiences of a large number of managers with acquisition exposure. Additional comments are shown underneath each section in italics.

Momentum toward completing a deal often builds despite the additional deci-sion-making hurdles put in place for acquisitions. The acquisition process is frequently described as having 'a life of its own' characterised by alternating periods of waiting and frenetic activity. As the tension, pace, and involvement rise relentlessly, participants tend to feel unable to stop the acquisition pro-cess or even slow its tempo. . . . This sense of inexorable momentum contrasts sharply with the traditional portrayal of acquisitions as carefully calculated strategic acts.

P.C. Haspeslagh and D.B. Jemison, *Managing Acquisitions*

Clarify the deal rationale – do's

1. Understand the reason for and underlying pressure driving the ven-dor.

2. Be clear what it is that you are getting.

3. The 'walk-away from' price must allow a good margin of worth to you of the deal.

Although these are three simple points, they should be branded on the foreheads of the acquisition team.

Track the deal fundamentals – do's

1. Know your 'tradables' in advance of the negotiation.

2. Get early agreement on the essentials.

3. Keep ongoing track of the benefits (value) of the deal and total costs of the deal as any changes occur.

These three points need continual work and a great deal of stamina. In particular, you cannot assume that the accountant on the team can necessarily capture all the implications of fast-moving negotiations in real time.

Managing the deal process – do's

1. Hold a pre-negotiation meeting(s) before deal-making with your advisers.

2. Remember that the deal is a learning process: you may learn things which cast new light on (a) attractiveness of the target, (b) attractiveness of the deal and (c) potential post-acquisition management difficulties.

3. Establish a series of check points at key stages to stand back and take an objective look at the proposition.

4. Take time out from negotiations if a log-jam exists and go back to essentials/tradables.

Because of the momentum that the deal process acquires, you need to invest considerable effort to manage the process in a calm, structured way.

Managing the communication process – do's

1. Work hard at communication – within 'the team' and with the vendor.

2. Focus all information through one key point.

3. Be absolutely clear on who has the final say.

These points are again easier said than done. Acquisition negotiations can become extremely complex and the opportunities for mis-communication abound. These opportunities are multiplied further with cross-border acquisitions where at least one side works in a second language.

Managing the relationships with the vendor – do's

1. Keep on thinking 'I am not here to make friends'.

2. Have a 'negotiation game plan' in place in advance – especially to give advantage over an unsophisticated/inexperienced vendor.

3. Exploit disagreement or fragmentation of views in the opposition.

4. Where an unsophisticated vendor is involved, be prepared to provide support:

    – to talk them through the key stages in advance;

    – when it all begins to seem 'too much' at later stages.

5. Avoid alienating key managers you wish to retain.

6. Make provision for continuity of employment, systems, etc., where you are buying part, not all, of a business.

It is not possible to offer rigid prescriptions in the area of managing relationships – essentially these should be managed on a situation-by-situation basis. However, the above six points flag up some important pointers.

Achieving tactical advantage – do's

1. Look for skeletons (by continual probing).

2. Be prepared to 'go for the extra' at the last stage of negotiations (the vendor's emotions take over here).

3. Reflect on your negotiating skills and style, and its strengths and weaknesses before finalizing the team.

4. Encourage candour from managers of the target.

5. Keep out of any areas clouded by lots of subjectivity on the part of vendors.

6. Be aware of who thinks they are driving the deal but without necessarily letting them influence the out-turn of negotiations (you can still be proactive!).

7. Be prepared to use financial tools as both valuation tools and as negotiating weapons.

Obviously point 2 needs to be weighed against the situation – late, deal-wrecking tactics are not being advocated here. Point 5 stresses the need to avoid getting into debates that involve lots of feeling about what the business might be worth – always go back to the strategic, financial and other facts.

Managing the acquisition team – do's

1. Appoint an 'acquisition project leader' (and, if necessary, a manager – to co-ordinate detailed information flows).

2. Involve 'the integrator' at key stages – indeed, consider making the integrator the project leader.

3. Ensure that the maximum experience of acquisitions is within the team, e.g. where the leader lacks 'experience' this needs to be counterbalanced.

4. Adjust your normal duties – it is not a part-time job.

5. Control the players in the team and the commitment 'up to the top'.

The organizational issues surrounding acquisition teams cause endless debate, often of a heated variety. It is imperative that roles and responsibilities are very well defined, otherwise there is a very real threat of going down the slippery slope into political in-fighting (points 1, 2 and 5). Also, point 4 actually means what it says – you can't lead a complex acquisition effectively at the peaks of activity alongside a heavy operational role – something has to give.

Deal-making don'ts

Managing the deal process – don'ts

1. Assume that your professional advisers individually know 'the whole picture'.

2. Allow ambiguity to persist in key areas, particularly in leaving it until too late to raise key legal, tax, pension or related issues.

3. See the deal in any sense as 'final and agreed' until formal closure.

The final point is critical – as soon as you think you have 'won' you may well have lost – in shareholder value terms.

Managing relationships with the vendor – don'ts

1. Get involved socially with vendor and representatives without a clear strategy (particularly for the inexperienced).

2. Give vague assurances of continuity of employment which you may not wish to be held to.

These points speak for themselves. Sometimes experienced acquirers greet point 1 with incredulity. But it does happen. Situations have occurred where an acquisition manager and the vendor's representative even swapped stories about their mistresses – maybe this was harmless intimacy, or maybe it was not.

Achieving tactical advantage – don'ts

1. Put all of your cards 'up front' on the table (be prepared to ask them what they are looking for – depending on the context).

2. Be stampeded by artificial deadlines.

3. Become impatient with apparent haggling over minutiae – this can be very important and have a big impact on value.

4. Give in to the temptation of 'giving in to' perfectly sound arguments without a fight.

5. Conceal skeletons where it will be evident you have been obviously manipulative as the concealment will be transparent.

Points 1–5 above again appear self-evident, but remember acquisitions can become very much an emotional experience where reason gets left behind unintentionally.

Managing the acquisition team – don'ts

1. Let any of your team display excessive enthusiasm.

2. Air your team disagreements in front of the opposition.

These issues are picked up very quickly by an experienced opposition, especially through unconscious, non-verbal behavior.

We turn now to the legal and tax issues. Legal and taxation complexities complicate the evaluation of the deal (a fundamentally sound 'business deal' can be negated or made marginal by contingent, legal liabilities, or because of the tax situation). Detailed legal and tax advice is often sought too late as the bid is made without clear attachment to exact conditions.

As deals are often set against deadlines (whether false or real), the negotiation process may run around the clock. The over-eager, acquisition champion may be tempted to cave in out of frustration and keenness to make headway.

It is intrinsically difficult to beat the market and strike a favourable deal without superior information. Moreover, the chances are that the buyer's information will be inferior, not superior, to that possessed by the seller. Hence we should not be surprised that many acquisitions are made at prices that destroy value for the buyer. Divestments, on the other hand, are more likely to be value creating; and we would observe that most parents look back with more pride on their divestment decisions than on their acquisitions.

M. Gould, A. Campbell and M. Alexander, *Corporate-level Strategy*

Funding issues are of paramount importance in doing the deal, and we therefore turn to these next.

Funding the Acquisition

This short section explores some of the main methods of funding acquisitions that the acquisition champion needs to consider.

The main method of funding acquisitions is via cash. From the vendor's point of view, cash is usually more desirable, as this will enable the vendor to use this economic resource for other strategic purposes. Also, it could be argued that otherwise the vendor would be dependent upon the new owners and their managers for future value creation – depending upon future share price performance.

Only where the acquirer's own prospects for shareholder wealth generation exceed the stock-market in general would it seem attractive to take the purchase consideration mainly in shares.

From an acquirer's point of view, use of shares as part or all of the purchase consideration conserves cash resource and limits gearing. This enables further acquisitions to be made – or other organic development. Where a public limited company is acquiring private companies it may be possible to produce some increase in apparent shareholder wealth by buying up companies with lower price–earnings ratios relative to your own, as we see in the example on the next page.

The problems with relying upon the above method of acquiring companies is that (a) once a number of acquisitions are done (or one of any

Smart things about funding strategies

- Beat the cost of capital (easily) for that kind of target.
- Avoid high-risk financial instruments when making higher risk acquisitions.

size), financial analysts may see through the artificial nature of this financial engineering – unless the company can genuinely produce some synergies; and (b) were the stock market to fall significantly, vendors might find it less attractive to receive shares (otherwise known as 'paper').

Besides shares and cash, there are a number of other methods of payment which include loan stock, preference shares or a deferred payment (based on performance criteria being met).

Deferred consideration helps to mitigate the risk that the acquired company may under-perform. This is often called an 'earn-out' arrangement where at least part of the purchase consideration is contingent upon future earnings post-acquisition. The problems with earn-outs is that it restricts the autonomy of the acquirer to adopt the company's strategy. Also, if the vendor's former owner stays on in a management capacity, the fact that he/she may now be somewhat rich might blunt their entrepreneurial drive.

BMW and Rover

Our continuing case study of BMW's acquisition of Rover Group in 1994 now illustrates how the process can easily become subservient to the acquirer's drive to consummate the deal.

British Aerospace had put itself in the position of *having* to sell Rover Group as a result of a weakening of both its civil and military aerospace markets (due to the ending of the Cold War). In addition, its new Chief Executive (who was previously Finance Director at BTR, the financially aggressive industrial conglomerate) took a highly commercial stance to BAe's future – its businesses needed to demonstrate their contribution to creating shareholder value (these factors reduced BAe's acquisition bargaining power). Finally, Rover Group needed considerable capital investment in its product development and production facilities, which BAe as a corporate parent was both unable and unwilling to provide; while BMW had spotted this opportunity, it would appear that Honda had not. In that respect BMW had been good at monitoring the availability of acquisitions and had been skilful in pre-empting any bid by Honda.

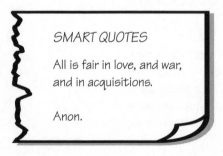

The following account is a summary of industry commentary at the time:

BMW offers Rover a new home

The deal process as at 1 February 1994 . . .

With £800 million on the table from BMW, it took

the British Aerospace board less than five hours to decide that it would exit the car industry and put an end to its five-year relationship with Honda.

Mr George Simpson, Rover's Chairman and the man who believed the relationship with Honda to be 'the natural path', was told by BAe to take the next flight to Tokyo to face a company which had thought its offer was a *fait accompli*. Six days earlier Honda had agreed to increase its stake from 20 to 47.5 per cent, pumping £165 million into BAe and valuing Rover at £600 million – 40 per cent less than the eventual winner. Honda had started from a seemingly unassailable position, given its 20 per cent stake and its fourteen-year relationship with Rover. But ultimately, it was BAe's desire to find an exit from its five-year-old investment that proved the key.

BMW had done a thorough job in stalking Rover: BMW had identified Rover in September 1993 as a target that would extend its car range and achieve economies of scale in distribution, component sourcing and R&D.

Its initial offer to BAe was repulsed because of Rover's relationship with Honda. Dr Hagen Luderitz, director of corporate planning at BMW, said that BMW delivered a letter to Honda chief executive Mr Nobuhiko Kawamoto, stating its interest in Rover. Strangely, no response was received.

Mr Kiyoshi Ikemi, councillor to Honda's president, denied any direct approach, claiming Honda received only indirect hints of BMW's intentions. 'We weren't informed properly until Friday last week', he protested.

By that time BMW had performed detailed operations due diligence on Rover: unperturbed by the original rebuff, BMW went ahead with its scrutiny of Rover. Mr Wolfgang Reitzle, BMW's research and development director, visited the UK plants and test drove the entire fleet. After two months, he decided that BMW had enough support to make a bid.

After BMW entered the competition, Honda responded rapidly. Having been informed of BMW's interest in Rover, Honda was under pressure. 'If we took a larger percentage, BAe said it would be a clear signal that the rest of the company was not for sale', said Mr Ikemi.

On 21 January, Honda agreed to increase its stake to 47.5 per cent. This offer was also before the BAe board on the Thursday morning.

BMW increased its offer to what was felt would be a knock-out blow, but it was a fierce race to the finish. Mr Luderitz admitted that the speed of the deal limited BMW's ability to perform due diligence, although he was confident the synergies with BMW justified the £800 million price tag – valuing Rover at £1 billion. He delivered the formal offer personally on 26 January.

At 9.15 a.m. on the following morning, the BAe board of directors made their decision. Before them was the prospect of selling a business that was seen as non-core and required substantial capital injection. The BMW offer had a deadline of midnight last night. The BAe board decided it wanted out – and Mr Simpson travelled to Tokyo to see if Honda would make a better offer, thus playing off both potential acquirers against each other. Honda decided that it did not want full control (at a price which beat the BMW offer).

According to commentary at the time, Honda's president, Nobuhiko

Kawamoto was visibly startled by BMW's revised bid. He protested, insisting that BAe had already agreed to sell Honda an additional 27.5 per cent stake in the Rover operating company, lifting its total to 47.5 per cent, and that they had a 'done-deal'.

Simpson explained that he was sorry, but Western businesses had to deal with issues such as stakeholder value, and in that context it was extremely difficult to evaluate things like a fifteen-year partnership and moral commitments. When the sums were done the bird in the hand – the £800 million – was worth much more than what Honda had offered.

Mr Kawamoto telephoned George Simpson at his hotel two hours later to say that there would be no deal on that basis.

When BMW originally began talks with Rover it offered around £550 million (*The Sunday Times*, 6 February 1994). But this figure was considerably less than Rover's book value of nearly £1.3 billion. Initially BMW made formal suggestions to Honda to co-operate in a Rover–BMW deal that would preserve the Honda–Rover link by direct association with BMW, thus mixing a acquisition with a continued alliance. According to *The Sunday Times* (6 February 1994), Mr Kawamoto did not reply to this proposal.

Honda's offer of £167 million to increase its stake from 20 to 47.5 per cent valued Rover Group at about £650 million. This was beaten on two counts by a BMW offer in January 1994 of around £700 million (for total control).

Then, on 16 January 1994, two Rover senior managers flew to Munich to meet BMW to enable BMW to make a full bid for the whole of

Rover – for Rover's holding company (and not just the subsidiary, in which Honda had a 20 per cent stake). It was at this point that BMW went for the knock-out punch.

When the offer finally arrived at BAe's London office (at 5 p.m. on Wednesday, 26 January) it had now been increased to £800 million – but after 1 February the bid would be withdrawn.

The core bid value of £800 million looked generous when tacked up against Rover's recent track record of pre-tax losses in 1991 and 1992 of around £50 million, and a pre-tax profit of merely £50 million in 1993. A price tag of £800 million indicated that BMW saw considerable incremental strategic (and ultimately) financial benefits flowing through from Rover. These benefits can be seen (with hindsight) to have been elusive.

Even though BMW had out-manoeuvred Honda it still had another hurdle to jump. George Simpson and Bernt Pischetsrieder, BMW's Chief Executive, both saw Tim Sainsbury, the UK industry minister, to press their case. Tim Sainsbury was persuaded on the argument that Rover would be unattractive to private shareholders with the continuing involvement of a minority shareholder, Honda, which had control of Rover's engine technology. (This is an interesting example of a strength in one argument being turned during the deal-making process into a weakness in another, to positive advantage.)

That BAe got a good price for Rover Group is undeniable. *The Sunday Times* (8 August 1993) foresaw (based on informed industry comment) that Rover would be sold for £400–500 million plus debt, just over half the BMW price tag.

Smart lessons from BMW deal-making process with Rover

- There is an inevitable trade-off between the need to conduct thorough operational due diligence and the need to head off competing bids. Nevertheless, the rush to close the deal may not allow for sufficient reflection and dispassionate critique of the target so that an inappropriate deal is struck.

- Where competition exists it is essential to perform scenarios for the deal-making process, e.g. if we make move X, will they make a move Y, and do we then make move Z and so on.

- The would-be acquirer needs to monitor potential acquisition targets continuously, not merely in terms of their performance and potential, but also in terms of the likely enthusiasm and pressure for sale. BMW achieved this very well, Honda not so well.

- When there is competition in the frame, it is very easy to pay to much for the deal. While a price tag of £800 million on profits of £50 million does not seem extravagant (in price–earnings ratio terms), if the deal were looked at in more prudent cash flow terms, the huge underlying investment need of Rover would have made it very hard indeed to justify a positive NPV of this order.

- Acquisition valuation is complex, and is not really an objective process – the valuation of Rover depended on (a) what you took on board, and what you divested of (now and in the future); (b) considerable future downsides (e.g. massive investment needed); and (c) the relative bargaining power and pressure to do a deal with all of the key players.

Summary

Acquisition deal-making is a crucial part of getting the value ('V2') out of the acquisition process. This involves second-guessing the agendas of the seller (or of the buyer), and of any other companies who might be bidding for your target.

The deal-making process and how it is conducted substantially determines the extent to which 'V2' (the value created, diluted or destroyed during the deal) is positive overall or negative. The first step in managing the deal-making process is to reflect upon the relative bargaining power of the acquirer versus the vendor in doing a deal.

This requires thinking through, for example, the number and flexibility of options that both parties have – and their relative time pressure to consummate a deal.

The key agendas underpinning acquirer and vendor behaviour also need careful thinking through, particularly to generate some story-lines (scenarios) of the dynamics of the deal. A number of deal-making do's and don'ts also need to be thought about in order to prevent errors – especially for the inexperienced. There may also be considerable variety of financing options, too, which also need to be carefully evaluated.

8

Acquisition Integration

The role of the acquisition champion

The integration phase is crucial for the acquisition champion as it is here where value is often diluted or destroyed rather than created. This may be due to a variety of reasons. For instance:

- New management might impose its own way of doing things and thus damage the acquisition's competitive strength. (At Rover Group, BMW imposed its own notion of what 'Britishness' was about, mispositioning the brand.)

- There may be an abrupt change in management style, leading to lower morale and business performance rather than improved performance.

- Integration plans may be left to emerge and, if deliberate, are inadequately thought through to deal with obstacles to change.

> Once the negotiations have been brought to a successful conclusion, the acquisition should be integrated with determination, and as fast as possible according to a predetermined plan, using as the spearhead a project team with membership from both companies. The aim must be to maximize the value of the enlarged enterprise, through the early realisation of the anticipated synergies, whilst at the same time minimising the inevitable impact of culture shock on the acquired company. Since culture shock of some kind is inevitable, it should be anticipated and mechanisms put in place to stimulate and motivate the key members of the acquired company, thereby giving them the personal incentive to deal effectively with their own culture shock in a positive manner.
>
> D. Faulkner and C. Bowman, *The Essence of Competitive Strategy*

- Alternatively, there may be no real change in the management when one is badly needed, leading to drift (as at Rover during 1995–1996).

- The acquisition period itself is a distracting time for incumbent management. There may be a period of months or longer when new developments are deferred, costs are unwisely cut. During this period the normal attention to customer delivery may be lost.

- Key staff may leave, feeling (rightly or wrongly) that their career prospects are blunted.

The integration phase is important as it is during this period that the acquirer has most opportunity to learn from the acquisition. This learning should obviously deal with the post-acquisition performance of the acquisition – financially and strategically. But it should also cover the acquisition process itself. How difficult and speedily did we integrate the acquisition relative to our expectations – is a central question.

In this chapter the reasons why integration strategies may fail and succeed, are examined, along with the pros and cons of different acquisition integration styles. The need to maintain business continuity is then addressed. This leads on to the need for the acquisition champion to project manage integration and the associated organizational issues. The need to monitor and learn from performance is then highlighted, and the links to post-acquisition learning and review.

The role of the acquisition champion during integration is thus to:

- Ensure that V3 (integration value) is captured, rather than destroyed.
- Determine the most appropriate style for integration management, depending on the context.
- Project manage the integration.
- Monitor achievement of organizational goals – short and longer term.
- Distil the learning from the acquisition – and feed this into future acquisition strategies and process.

Integration success and failure

Acquisition integration can fail for a large number of reasons. Figure 8.1 captures these reasons as a 'fishbone' analysis. Using the fishbone, the key symptom of the problem is shown at the right-hand side of the page – at the fish's head. The underlying root causes of the problem are depicted as the bones of the fishbone. (Note the there is no special order to the fishbone analysis display.)

Figure 8.1 highlights some of the main reasons for failure. These range from there not being an effective and robust strategy in the very first place through to inadequate integration planning and project manage-

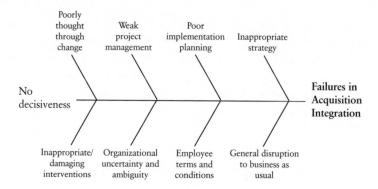

Figure 8.1 A "fishbone" analysis of failures in acquisition integration.

ment and inappropriate organizational change. Typically, unsuccessful integration processes are characterized by a lack of decisiveness on the part of the acquiring management team or through inappropriate and damaging interventions.

After deciding 'who does what' in the new organization, the second most difficult stumbling block is likely to be around employee terms and conditions. Unilateral changes to salary structures and to benefits in kind just after the acquisition are likely to trigger significant disruption in the organizational process.

SMART QUOTES

Strategic vision is where all acquisitions begin. Management's vision of the acquisition is shared with suppliers, customers, lenders, and employees as a framework for planning, discussions, decisions, and reactions to changes. The vision must be clear to large constituent groups and adaptable to many unknown circumstances.

M.L. Sirower, The Synergy Trap

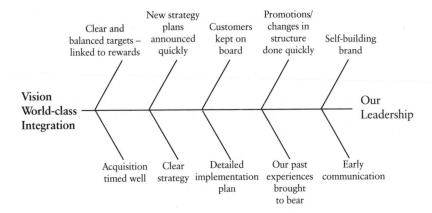

Figure 8.2 A "wishbone" analysis of successes in acquisition integration.

It is useful to examine (at a more positive level) what factors would need to line up to deliver a particularly effective implementation process. This is depicted in Figure 8.2. Notice that while some of these alignment factors are reversals of the fishbone analysis, some of them are not, and all of them are not in any way average, but more superior or visionary.

Figure 8.2 thus emphasizes the importance of having a best-in-class integrative process, with scenario story-telling, excellent integration project management and a balanced set of performance measures.

Integration strategies – the alternatives

Integration strategies can range along a continuum, from:

leave well alone → put managers in to complement the team →
install a substantially new management team

The acquisition champion obviously has choices too as to the speed of
the intervention during integration. Changes can be implemented
immediately, or after a period of say six to nine months, or perhaps after
around eighteen months.

Where management skills are felt by the acquisition champion to fall
significantly short of needs, it is not a good idea at all to delay action
putting in additional management skills. Often a leave-alone or wait-
and-see approach may lead to disappointing post-acquisition performance.

Organizational morale can easily go into a downward spiral during integration, especially where there are delays in agreeing new structures and

Smart approaches to integration

- If you think you are going to need to make changes, do this as soon as possible –
do not procrastinate.
- The decision as to what extent you do need to make changes depend very much
on:
  - current management's strengths and weaknesses
  - flexibility (or lack of it) of current management's mind-set
  - the requirements of the future business strategy and its associated competitive challenges.
- The value which you feel you can add to the acquisition, and your own team's
existing competencies
- The amount of available management skills which you have, and the opportunity
cost of deploying them on this particular acquisition.

roles. This can be represented in Figure 8.3, where morale over time is plotted against organizational performance over time.

Ironically, while acquisitions are bought ostensibly in order to generate *increased* performance, in the short run performance typically declines – due to organizational fear. Where an experienced acquirer is involved the opposite effect is frequently created: the integration situation gives management a new clarity and sense of challenge (as it once did at Hanson plc in its boom years).

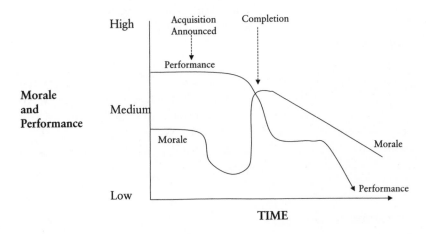

Figure 8.3 Integration dynamics.

In addition to management changes (and associated structures), a second important and difficult area for the champion to manage is organizational routines, processes and procedures. For although these may seem less crucial, they form an integral part of the culture of the organization. Changes to these can irritate and alienate current staff, especially if new processes are perceived to be inferior to the old.

A useful approach is to define best practices for the new organization based on the best of the acquired business and the acquirer – and on best practices generally.

One area of particular sensitivity is that of change in management reporting systems. While change (to the new group) may not be negotiable, it may be wise to allow some limited transition period to allow the acquired company a little more time to get used to getting its returns in more quickly, and in compliance with group accounting procedures. This transition should be discussed and agreed *before*, and not after completion.

The final thing to reflect upon in this area is: What sort of integration strategy does the particular situation naturally lend itself to? For example, if your target is in need of significant turnaround, then you will need well-honed commercial skills and change management skills to become truly successful. These might well be skills that you – as an acquirer – do not possess in abundance.

Communication issues

Besides keeping management and staff up to speed with the changes associated with the acquisition, you will also need to communicate with

KILLER
QUESTIONS

Organizational structure

- For a potential acquisition you are considering:
- What are the skills gaps within the existing management structure?
- What skills do you have within your organization to fill these gaps, or what skills do you need to buy in from elsewhere?
- Which staff could be developed from within the acquired company to fill these gaps?
- When is it best to make these changes?
- How are you going to position these changes in the company – to avoid unnecessary disillusionment.
- Are there any key positions that you will want to change anyway?

---

customers and suppliers. This means not merely spelling out the *fact* of the acquisition, but also the implications for them. Failure to do this can materially weaken the external network of other companies that the company is reliant upon.

Consider the following illustration from the Rover case . . .

Rover's disposal by BMW in 2000 to Phoenix

In early 2000 Rover Cars (excluding the four-wheel-drive business and the Mini) was acquired from BMW by a consortium of investors led by John Towers, former Chief Executive of Rover. Previously, Rover's future had been highly uncertain and its alternative acquirer, Alchemy Partners, a venture capital group, planned to run down production from around 150,000–200,000 units per annum to just 50,000.

When Phoenix succeeded in buying Rover Cars, its new owners

announced plans that it intended to produce 200,000 units per annum in future. Its suppliers took this quite seriously and at face value. In mid/late 2000 when their expected level of orders failed to materialize, Rover MG (the new company) announced that the 200,000 figure was merely a forecast. This obviously had a big and disappointing impact on Rover's suppliers.

Communication with customers is equally important, too. Examine this next example:

Post-acquisition management – the case of the vanishing customer

A large food company acquired one of its major competitors. The integration value V3 was intended to come from a combination of cost savings and from improved pricing with its key customers. By capturing more market share, it was hoped that the company's bargaining power would increase, and it would be able to avoid discounting on longer-term contracts.

Once the food company had been acquired, one of its major customers (who had not been born yesterday) promptly switched its sourcing to other suppliers. The food company lost – overnight – around £50 million of sales.

During the integration phase it is therefore imperative to establish a detailed communication plan to deal with the expectations of key stakeholders.

Government and regulatory stakeholders can also be important, as the following example at BMW–Rover highlights:

BMW suffers amnesia – and forgets the British government

In early 2000 BMW finally succumbed to the costs of post-acquisition losses at Rover Group. Approached by venture capital firm Alchemy, BMW agreed a deal to dispose of Rover's loss-making business – with major sweeteners as a pay-off. (The four-wheel-drive business was to be sold to Ford).

Whether by accident or design, BMW omitted to tell the British government of its plan. When the news was broken on television the Labour Government was absolutely livid that they had been kept in the dark over this deal. UK television was dominated by the news for forty-eight hours afterwards.

The UK government had just cause to be angry as they had provided significant investment grants to BMW Rover to help fund new model launches.

The cost of the proposed deal with Alchemy was that BMW fell out of favour with the government, sales of BMWs fell in the UK (BMW's number one export market) and BMW had to pay Alchemy compensation for switching the sale to rival bidders Phoenix.

To establish a full communication plan you will need to think through the following:

- Customer communication, including
  - telephone calls (preferably)
  - follow-up letters
  - selected meetings (very soon indeed after completion)
- Supplier communication (as above)
- Distributors (as above)

- Management and staff
  - the letter (of the initial announcement)
  - meetings/presentations (in the first week post-completion)
  - individual interviews/meetings (within the first few weeks following completion)
- Government and regulating authorities
  - Selective communication, dependent upon potential impact.

You can see from the above that there is a great deal of work to do in the intermediate period following completion. This is likely to come very soon after the equally busy period of the negotiations. Management attention and effort can droop in the early post-acquisition phase and begin to destroy V3.

KILLER
QUESTIONS

Post-acquisition communication

For a hypothetical acquisition which you might purchase:
- Who do you need to communicate to
  - before completion?
  - on completion day?
  - -in the first week following completion?
  - -in the first month following completion?
- What do you need to communicate?
- How is communication best accomplished?

Project managing integration

A 'project' is sometimes defined as being *a complex set of activities that aim to deliver a pre-determined result at a pre-planned time and cost.*

Acquisition integration is certainly complex, goal orientated, costly and also takes significant time – it is certainly a project. Yet this needs to be project managed explicitly by the acquisition champion.

Acquisition integration is not a single project, but comprises of many projects. These include, for example:

- Restructuring
- Product development decisions
- Recruitment
- Cost reduction programmes
- Name change/brand repositioning
- IT systems alignment
- Financial reporting integration

The task force should include someone who may be asked to play a substantial management role after the acquisition. With such a manager on the task force integration issues are more likely to be given careful attention before the decision is made. In addition the acquiring firm is better able to retain the understanding, respect, and authority that build up during the often lengthy negotiating process.

P.C. Haspeslagh and D.B. Jemison, *Managing Acquisitions*

SMART QUOTES

- Disposal of parts of business

- Closures

- Customer retention

- Employee communication

- Management development and training

- Culture change and team-building

- Further business strategy development (last but not least)

and so on . . .

Each project will require:

- Key deliverables

- Prioritization

- Time-scales

- Resourcing

- Activity analysis (key activities, timescales and interdependencies)

- A business case

- Uncertainty analysis

This can be achieved through mini-project plans, rather than this developing into a bureaucracy. A good role of thumb is to draw these up to be between three and five pages for each project. Each project is also likely to have interdependencies *vis-à-vis* other projects. The really key interdependencies between projects need to be mapped out.

There needs to be as many project managers as there are projects. A good role of thumb is for each member of the senior management team to have (ideally) no more than three integration projects to work on. See the panel below that describes a smart integration team.

Notice that in the smart acquisition team there does not have to be an

A smart integration team

Managing Director
- Further strategy development
- Employee communication
- Culture change and team-building

Marketing Director
- Name change/brand positioning
- Customer retention
- Product development decisions

Operations Director
- Cost reduction decisions
- Closures

IT Director
- IT systems alignment

HR Director
- Restructuring
- Recruitment
- Management development and training

Financial Director
- Financial reporting
- Disposal of parts of business

obvious alignment between functional responsibilities and project definition. So, for example, the Managing Director can perfectly well deal with employee communication and culture change and team-building: this does not necessarily have to be the domain of the HR Director. Also, a commercially rounded Financial Director ought to be able to manage some business disposals. Cost reduction might be better *not* to be allocated to the Financial Director as this may seem to be a finance-led initiative, rather than cross-functional.

In order to assist with project planning, you will need to use a number of project management techniques (which are now explained), namely:

- Attractiveness –implementation difficulty ('AID' analysis)

- How–how analysis

- Urgency – important analysis

- Gantt chart analysis

- Stakeholder analysis

It is perfectly possible to find an integration project that is attractive and which also has clear benefits, and yet is extremely difficult to implementent. Alternatively, a project may be relatively easily implemented, but not particularly attractive or beneficial.

The attractiveness–implementation tool ('AID' grid) enables these

Smart things to know about AID analysis

- It can prioritize acquisition targets
- And integration strategies
- And specific integration projects

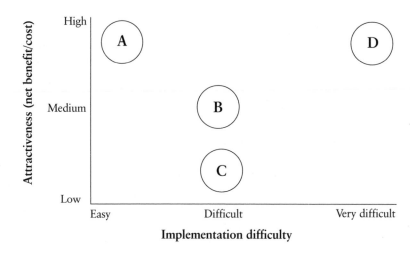

Figure 8.4 Attractiveness/implementation difficulty (AID) analysis.

trade-offs to be achieved. This tool enables a portfolio of possible integration projects to be prioritized. Figure 8.4 illustrates a hypothetical
case.

Integration project A is seen as being both very attractive and relatively
easy to implement. This project is non-contentious and will probably be
given the go-ahead. Project B is somewhat more difficult. It is only moderately attractive and is difficult. Project B requires a good deal of
testing of the net benefits (is it really that attractive – would it be much
harder than we currently think?).

Integration project C is relatively difficult – it will probably end up being
zapped unless it can be reformulated to make it both a lot more attractive and easier.

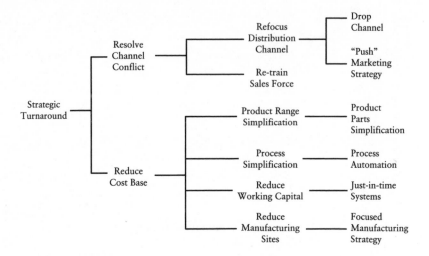

Figure 8.5 How–How analysis: acquisition integration at Skil Corporation, USA.

Integration project D presents the biggest dilemma of all. Although it appears to be very attractive it is also very difficult to implement. Yet managers will tend to focus on the attractiveness of the project rather then its actual difficulty.

The How–How picture (see Figure 8.5) now helps us to break down the integration programme (and projects) into subsections. We are then able to assess how important and urgent these are.

How–How analysis can now be used to work through the detailed implications posed by acquisition integration. For instance, in a now famous Harvard Business School case study, Michael Porter describes how a US corporation, Skil, a power tools business, tried to achieve a turnaround strategy following its acquisition.

This strategy had two main planks: refocusing distribution channels and reducing Skil's cost base in an attempt to become market leader. Implicitly, Skil management worked out the logic of implementation unconsciously using a 'How–How' approach. The key ingredients of this implementation strategy can now be depicted through the How–How methodology (see Figure 8.5). How–How can act as a very fruitful brainstorming tool to encourage managers to think through (in a progressive degree of detail) the implications of the integration strategy.

The 'importance' and 'urgency' grid (Figure 8.6) now invites the question of 'important to whom and why?' (hopefully to the business). It may also result in questioning the degree of perceived urgency. Finally,

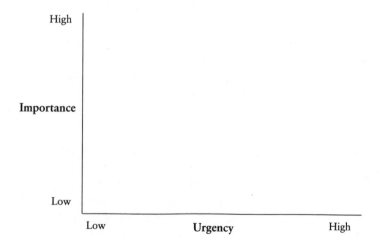

Figure 8.6 Urgency–importance grid.

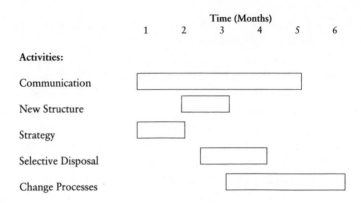

Figure 8.7 Gantt chart analysis: post-acquistion integration.

importance and urgency analysis can be used to map separate acquisition integration projects *and their interdependence* pictorially – as a prelude to planning the critical path(s) within a complex integration.

The Gantt chart (Figure 8.7) is a way of taking the activities from the How–How picture and plotting acquisition activities over time as a bar diagram. This needs to be checked for feasibility in terms of (a) timescales for activities and (b) resources availability.

Stakeholder analysis (Figure 8.8) is the systematic identification of key stakeholders and appraisal of their influence on, and posture towards acquisition integration. It may also involve creating a strategy to reshape the influence of these or new stakeholders. A 'stakeholder' is defined as someone with an influence over an integration decision, over its implementation or who is merely a victim of the integration project.

1. Identify who you believe the key stakeholders are at any phase of the process (the 'stakeholder brainstorm').

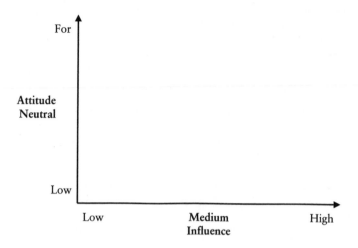

Figure 8.8 Stakeholder analysis.

2. Evaluate whether these stakeholders have high, medium or low influence on the issue in question. (You need to abstract this from their influence generally in the organization.)

3. Evaluate whether at the current time they are for the project, against it, or idling in 'neutral'.

The above gives a good 'first cut' of the pattern of stakeholders. The cluster of stakeholders depicted on a stakeholder grid (see Figure 8.8) should then be assessed to see what the overall picture looks like, particularly:

• Is the integration project an easy bet?

• Or is it highlighting a long slog?

• Or, finally, does this seem like 'mission impossible'?

- It deals with the softer and the more political and challenging aspects of acquisitions.
- It enables you to continuously monitor shifts in stakeholder positionings, and to focus your influencing strategies.

Following the first-cut analysis, managers can then move on to the next phase:

1. Is it possible to boost the influence of stakeholders who are currently in favour of the change?

2. Is it possible to reduce the influence of antagonistic stakeholders?

3. Can new stakeholders be brought into play to shift the balance or can existing players be withdrawn in some way (or be subtly distracted)?

4. Can coalitions of stakeholders in favour be achieved so as to strengthen their combined influence?

5. Can coalitions of stakeholders antagonistic to the project be prevented?

6. Can the integration plan itself, in appearance or in substance, be reformulated to diffuse hostility to the project?

SMART QUOTES

Managers faced with a multitude of hurdles overcome them by selling (slightly) different views of the acquisition to different stakeholders in the hope of winning their support.

P.C. Haspeslagh and D.B. Jemison, *Managing Acquisitions*

7. Are there possibilities of 'bringing on board' negative stakeholders be allowing them a role or in incorporating one or more of their prized ideas?

Stakeholder analysis is essential to gain more ownership over acquisition integration. It embraces both internal and external stakeholders.

If you are still in doubt over the wisdom of employing project management process explicitly to integration, consider the following brief case:

Acquisition integration – achieving mission impossible with project management

A senior manager who was attending a strategic change programme at a major business school worked on some of his own business issues. Apparently he had been asked to integrate the operations of an about-to-be acquired manufacturing operation in Poland. The goal of this project was to make these operations 'world-class' within an eighteen-month time period.

Apparently this entailed cutting the current staff levels from 400 to 80 staff. Asked whether he had thought of applying project management processes to this task, he reflected: 'I never really thought of doing that, I saw this as an operational task which I could combine with my visits around the Eastern Bloc countries. I honestly had not seen this as a complex project.'

Thankfully, following this brief conversation, he did then recognize this as a 'project'.

Evaluating success

Once the acquisition champion has defined the integration strategy and has begun to manage the integration process through project management, the resulting performance needs to be monitored.

Conventionally this is done through monitoring short-term accounting profits. While these do of course need monitoring, equally important is delivering of shareholder value. To achieve this, this acquisition free cash flow should be monitored, by the acquisition champion on a quarterly/bi-annual basis. For example, reflecting on BMW's acquisition of Rover again, Rover's accounting losses began to mount only two years after the acquisition. But even in that time period the costs of investment in product development increased dramatically. Rover's 'free cash flow' (its operating net cash flows, less investment) showed a much more disturbing trend than the decline in conventional accounting profits.

To analyse performance more visually there are two major ways of understanding its underlying drivers through integration. These are:

• Performance driver analysis (external and internal)

• Fishbone analysis

In performance driver analysis the positive performance drivers are shown as upward arrows – whose length is a reflection of perceived importance and strength. The negative or downward facing arrows represent brakes in performance.

Figures 8.9 and 8.10 represent the drivers in external performance impacting on Rover during 1998–2000. Notice that the relative balance of these arrows is negative, suggesting major downward pressure on Rover's performance. Also the internal performance driver analysis (Figure 8.10) is even more depressing.

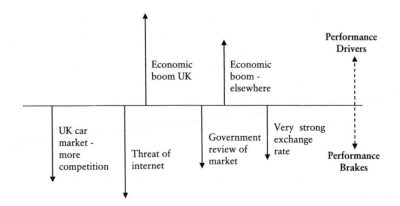

Figure 8.9 Performance drivers (external) – Rover 1998–2000.

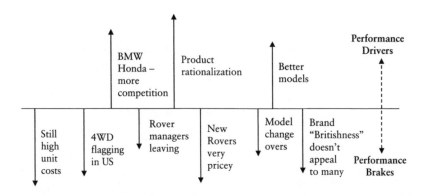

Figure 8.10 Performance drivers (internal) – Rover 1998–2000.

The 'so-what?' from this analysis is that:

• Substantial financial losses were imminent.

- Rover Group would require major surgery to survive, and even then it might not achieve this in anything like its current form.

- Phoenix would have an extremely tough job turning Rover around, and could quickly burn up its cash reserves (losses were around £300 million in its first year following the acquisition of Rover cars).

If you wish to go to a level deeper in the diagnosis, 'fishbone analysis' can help us to trail backwards from an adverse performance symptom to the underlying root causes. Here one starts to the right of the picture with the fish's head. The bones of the picture are the root causes of the problem. These root causes are identified by repeatedly asking the question 'Why is this a problem . . . ?'.

Figure 8.11 shows fishbone analysis for just one of Rover's performance brakes.

Although it is possible to combine the external and internal performance drivers within one picture, the disadvantage of that approach is

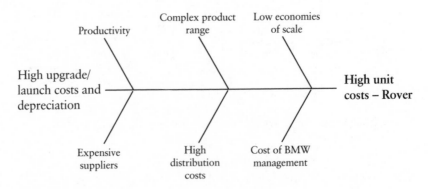

Figure 8.11 A performance brake – Rover 1998–2000.

that internal drivers tend to be focused on – to the detriment of external drivers.

Performance drivers and fishbone analysis should therefore be used in addition to conventional analysis of accounting profit and free cash flow to monitor ongoing acquisition performance.

Smart things to know about performance drivers

They give you an X-ray picture of business performance –and what is good/not so good

An integrated monitoring system for integration would therefore combine tracking of five key things:

- Accounting profits

- Free cash flow/shareholder value added

- The speed of integration projects

- Customer perception of the new company

- The level of organizational morale and energy.

The above five indicators can be tracked as an applied 'balanced-score card' for the success of the acquisition.

Post-acquisition learning and review

Most of the techniques for post-acquisition learning and review are now in place from the previous section. One can now readily reappraise the acquisition by examining a number of issues in the following killer questions.

Developing and diagnosing integration performance

- Has the acquisition delivered accounting profit targets?
- Has it delivered its free cash flow targets?
- What are the external and internal performance drivers, and what prognosis do these give for the acquisition's success?
- Have these drivers changed since the company was acquired and why? (Use fishbone analysis.)
- Did integration projects deliver on time and, if not, why not? (Use Fishbone analysis again.)
- What is customer's perception of the business and how has this changed since the pre-acquisition period?
- What is the level of organizational morale and energy in the organization?
- Given the above analysis, what changes to an integration strategy are now needed?

Summary

Acquisition integration often fails due to inexperience, a lack of resources or focus, and particularly because of poor integration management. Integration strategies need to be carefully evaluated – according to the context, although in general, 'hands-off' strategies frequently fail.

During the early integration period the acquisition champion will have his/her work cut out in communication exercises, and in setting up and steering the various integration projects. This is time intensive and is not a part-time job. Management of stakeholders is an especially critical part of this phase.

Delivering acquisition performance is very much a diagnostic, a learning and feedback process, rather than primarily a number-crunching exercise.

Acquisition learning checklists

- Did new, external brakes on performance crystallize, and what was their impact?
- Were our assumptions about lifecycle effects impacting on the acquisition's product range valid – and also their competition strengths and weaknesses?
- Were internal performance drivers managed as well as was hoped for, and did new internal brakes on performance materialize?
- Why did specific performance problems occur? (Fishbone analysis.)
- The integration projects – were these as attractive and as easy as was assumed?
- Were interdependencies managed as well as they needed to be?
- Were all the critical assumptions about the whole acquisition integration identified, and did we understand their importance/degree of uncertainty?
- Was brand strategy (post-integration) appropriate?
- Was the quality of target's management as good as what we thought?
- Were assumed investment levels to deliver V3 adequate or not?
- Did we lose key personnel by mishandling the softer issues (restructuring, management development, remuneration, perks, etc.)?
- Did the changes to key individuals in the management team work and well, and if not, why not?
- Did we intervene inappropriately in operational practices – causing unnecessary disruption?
- Were we really clever in defining our integration strategy and integration projects or did these change considerably in scope and difficulty over the first eighteen months?
- Did we devote enough time and attention to managing the acquisition integration?

9

The Champney's Case

Introduction and background

This acquisition case study on Champney's Health Resort illustrates for the acquisition champion many of the lessons covered in this integration section. It also links backwards to what was learnt about acquisition strategy and to operations due diligence. The case study allows a prospective acquisition champion to get a taste of the reality of acquisition strategy and integration – especially through organizational restructuring.

In particular, it reinforces lessons about:

- Defining your objectives in acquiring a business clearly at the outset.

- Diagnosing the strategic and financial health of target before making the acquisition.

- Considering more radical options for developing and integrating the company.

- Scoping the integration issues.

- Determining its future management and structure – in advance

- Anticipating the implementation difficulties.

- Scoping the 'iceberg' of future investment.

- Working out a game plan for 'where to go next' – following integration.

Champney's Health Resort is located at Tring, Hertfordshire, thirty miles or so from central London. Champney's is a select, rural retreat for its members, who principally reside in and around the Home Counties, England. Traditionally it is a most exclusive retreat, charging near-Savoy prices for its luxurious and relatively exotic services, which are to do with skincare and generally looking after the body.

Due to economic slowdown Champney's was suffering considerably. Falling demand meant that its cash flow had deteriorated to the point where it experienced an annual cash deficit which was approximate to accounting losses of £1 million on a turnover of £10 million. Its previous owners decided that enough was enough and sold the business to foreign investors.

In business terms, Champney's was in a strategic turnaround situation. Its new investors decided that a breath of life needed to be injected into Champney's to secure its future. At the same time, Champney's was saddled with a particular set of management behaviour, and this need to be challenged strongly by any new owners and management so that the organization could move forward.

Savoy-trained Lord Thurso was recruited to spearhead the recovery. Initially its new, Middle-Eastern owner wanted Lord Thurso to work at

Champney's on a non-executive basis. But through opening up the discussions with the owner, Lord Thurso discovered that with the scale of Champney's problems this would require a full-time involvement. Notably this appointment came *after* Champney's had been bought, and not before. As its new Chief Executive, Lord Thurso set about formulating an integration plan that would secure Champney's a viable future. At this time Champney's also featured in the BBC 2 television series *Trouble at the Top*. Some of the quotes from Lord Thurso given below are taken from the television programme, some from an interview.

In the tradition of turnaround specialists, Lord Thurso set himself a tight deadline for formulating his integration plan – just one month. In the course of that month, Lord Thurso was to spend the bulk of his time listening to Champney's various stakeholders, particularly:

• Members and regular customers

• Staff

• Current managers

Lord Thurso's early findings indicated that Champney's suffered from a number of underlying problems (see Figure 9.1, which portrays a 'fishbone', or 'root cause', analysis of its malaise). These included:

• A legacy of under-investment (and decay)

• A decline in standards generally

• An overly-zealous attempt to market Champney's time shares, to customers outside Champney's core customer base

• Promises made to members that could not be kept

• A top-heavy management structure

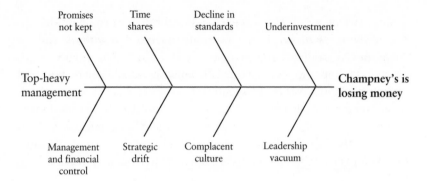

Figure 9.1 A "fishbone" analysis of Champney's situation.

- Relatively poor (or inappropriate) management and financial controls

- A lack of a sense of strategic direction generally

Instead of inheriting a strong business with a national potential for immediate expansion, Champney's new owner began to appreciate rapidly that to achieve his commercial goals at Champney's required radical surgery.

Lord Thurso, on his first inspection of the property after taking over, noted that:

> It is clearly very tired. These rooms would have been considered five star when they were built, but clearly the expectations of five star have changed. It is bland, it is grey, it is a very dead, dull room, it has no colour and it has zero on the excitement scale.   (BBC 2)

Also, Champney's strategic positioning itself seemed to be unclear:

I have asked the question of everybody 'What are we selling?' and I get a lot of long-winded answers; the real answer is that no one has thought about it.   (BBC 2)

He also reflected:

And I had also decided – it was as plain as day – that at the heart of the previous strategy, was this wonderful name 'Champney's', which was the great opportunity. But what had been created in the past was the infrastructure for a hundred million pound company, even though it was only ten million pound company.

It had all these people here who were called brand managers, and none of them understood what a brand was. And that was the extraordinary thing – none of them understood the elementary concept of a brand being a promise made to customers that has values and a character. If you said to them 'What does Champney's mean?', the answer was, they hadn't thought it through.   (Interview)

Many of these issues must have been apparent almost as soon as Lord Thurso drove up Champney's drive. As soon as he arrived, he found a mass of memos from his managers. Lord Thurso recalled:

There are piles and piles of paper. It is a fairly classic thing – there are too many managers sending memos to each other. And I am suspicious of any company that is capable of generating so much paper when they are told they are expecting a new Chief Executive.   (BBC 2)

He also reflected:

When I arrived here, there were huge reports on everything. I said to them 'Look, I just don't read them. I don't mind reading a novel by Tolstoy or Dick Francis, but I am not going to read *that*!'   (Interview)

At the same time, management lacked the fundamental information that it requires:

> We do not have good financial information. In fact, not only is it not good, it is actually awful. The management accounts that I have seen are mathematically correct but they are not informative.   (BBC 2)

He said later:

> There was a management structure which didn't work. The management reports were gibberish. I asked simple questions: 'Do you know what your cash flow is?' and the guy couldn't tell me. . . . They didn't produce balance sheets. They produced huge, thick reports, full of graphs, trend analysis. But the one thing that they didn't do was to produce reports where you could find profit, where you could find cash flow. I said we will really have to start from scratch.
> I remember sitting on the lawn on holiday wearing my Panama hat and a T-shirt and my kilt, and smoking a cigar trying to read through two years of drivel, the management accounts. . . . I can usually work things out and I just couldn't make it work.   (Interview)

However, instead of rolling out his acquisition integration plan straight away, Lord Thurso spent precious time soliciting the views of all the company's key stakeholders. This enabled him not only to be absolutely sure that his chosen path was the right one, but also that, in behavioural terms, it was owned.

This period of listening was also, in fact primarily, so Lord Thurso could establish a rapport with his new staff. He told me:

> To be honest, I had already made up my mind before I arrived here

what I would do. I had actually decided before the day that I started that I was going to take a million pounds out of the costs.   (Interview)

He continued:

> I wanted them to have thought that I had thought it through. They wouldn't have understood that I was capable of thinking it through very quickly, and that it was really clear what had to be done. It was really a very simple problem and it needed some pretty straightforward solutions.
>
> After I arrived I said, 'I will have a month and I will make no decision until the end of the month.' It was a good thing. I did fractionally amend certain decisions but 90 per cent of it was exactly what I had thought [previously].   (Interview)

Lord Thurso realized intuitively that Champney's was the kind of situation that could so easily blow up if a number of stakeholders decided, rightly or wrongly, that he was 'the wrong man for the job'. Quite quickly, Lord Thurso concluded from his own personal course of treatments that his operational staff were a real asset – to be retained, nurtured and grown:

> The closer I get to the front line, the better I find the troops are. And that is very pleasing because if you have good officers and lousy soldiers you have got a lot of work to do, but if you have good soldiers and lousy officers, then you have to work to train or change the officers.   (BBC 2)

In some contrast, Lord Thurso found the management that he had inherited, although up to the task of managing in a more steady-state environment, were not really up to a turnaround. The top-heavy management structure was not only an expense that the business could not afford, it also impeded the integration plan. In effect, Lord Thurso was carrying out the organizational and people due diligence which perhaps should be performed before completion.

Acquisition integration strategy – options

Champney's future strategy was thus developed in detail only after completion of the deal. Obviously, this was less than ideal as it is critical to have a clear view and details of that strategy *before* the acquisition.

However, given that Champney's was now under new ownership a number of options for acquisition integration strategy existed – see 'Smart options' listed below. To develop these options in greater detail would require using the Strategic Option Grid (see Chapter 2).

Smart options for Champney's

- Market positioning – especially in terms of degree of exclusivity (and pricing levels).
- Customer focus – in terms of customer segmentation and geographic location.
- Customer need – e.g. pampering versus health improvement.
- Product choice – duration of stay, mix and range of treatments, vehicle for delivering these.
- Facilities – lavish versus economical.
- Corporate development options – including alliances, franchising, further acquisitions.
- Organizational structure (as is, slimmed down, very lean).
- Resources (alternative combinations).

Champney's actual integration strategy (as determined by Lord Thurso) was to:

- Focus on a more exclusive market positioning, with customers coming from an hour or so's drive of its facility. These excluded corporate clients.

- Continue to focus on pampering treatments, while adding selectively to the range – delivered in a traditional way.

- Supported by a very considerable investment facilities of £6.75 million.

- And with a halving of the management team (from 22 to 11).

Other smart options for Champney's

Other integration options which were also available might have been:
- Market positioning which maintained pricing but was less narrowly 'exclusive' – opening it up to perhaps a younger age-range especially to successful high-income professionals wanting to 'chill-out'.
- Extending geographic reach beyond a medium-range drive to appeal, for example, to overseas visitors from the US, from Europe and from other countries, creating a truly international facility.
- Product development: making a regular (six-monthly) stay at Champney's compulsory – at a psychological level – as part of a whole set of lifestyle improvements, possibly supported by visiting therapists (in your own home) in the interim.
- Customer need: shifting the mix of treatments from beauty/pampering to total health and wellbeing treatments – 'Nowhere else makes you feel this great' was Champney's new mission statement. Also, including corporate clients in Champney's target customers, and an increased focus on men (and not just 'women and their partners').

- Facilities: these might have been upgraded perhaps with more modest spend, increasing Champney's role of return.
- Corporate development: active consideration of franchises overseas, and potentially a northern Champney's (by acquisition/organic development) perhaps at Harrogate, Yorkshire.
- Resources: subcontracting out of property management facilities and the sale of a plot of Champney's land for development of luxury flats, capitalizing on the property boom in the UK between 1997 and 2000. Potentially this might have released several million pounds of capital without reducing Champney's ambience.
- Brand: an alliance with a food company to exploit Champney's brand and its food recipes (perhaps coupled with an innovative TV chef series based at Champney's).
- Organization structure: instead of maintaining management levels at half of previous levels (eleven), actually reducing levels further to five–seven. (In fact, Champney's management team was down to seven by 2001 – even though Champney's had then expanded with additional facilities in central London and Brussels – showing that this was possible.)

The list of other smart options highlights that there is often considerable room for creative thinking when determining the integration strategy. This is a time for imagination and truly vigorous thinking about how more shareholder value can be created – and not just in terms of the existing business model.

Here, a central line of enquiry is still 'How do we exploit the Champney's brand', which was a key value driver within the integrated business.

The integration process

Having diagnosed the key organizational issues, Lord Thurso now faced

SMART QUOTES

a major dilemma: if he moved very fast and introduced a new, slimmed-down management structure, the shock might topple the organization, undermining morale at the cutting edge of customer service. In these situations, there is probably no single 'right answer'. Arguably, by leaving Champney's managers in suspense for one month, he prolonged the agony of uncertainty. On the other hand, by at least listening to them over this period he ensured he had a better idea of who was and was not able to make the transition – and also, in simple, financial terms, how many he could take with him.

Lord Thurso said:

> First of all, I wanted a huge change and I wanted that to sink in quickly. I wanted the troops, the army in the resort, to go 'Hey, this guy might know what he is talking about'!
> I also felt that I only wanted to do it once. I wanted it to be viciously quick for two reasons: one as to make a point, and the other thing was to say to people 'That's it. It is done.' And that undoubtedly worked.   (Interview)

Lord Thurso was thus alert to the need to preserve and enhance organizational morale during the most difficult phases of integration.

Once this first, crucial month was up, Lord Thurso needed to move fast to communicate and implement the first stages of his integration plan.

He reflected, subsequent to organizational changes, just how serious the problems at the old head office had become:

> And there was a business over there that had been completely neglected at head office. There was a flip chart in every office, which to me was a symptom of this very introverted style – the moment anybody had a meeting, someone was on a flip chart. The whole thing was driven by the processes rather than by the objectives. If there were objectives, they were tacked onto the process.
>
> People worked hard and interacted and interfaced, and essentially went round in circles. There was no questioning of 'Why are we here?' or 'What is the meaning of the universe?'
>
> It was quite clear that I had to make a very definitive statement that there was a complete change coming. It wasn't quite as bloody as it looked, because I redeployed quite a lot of the people I had here back into the units. That refocused them on where the action was.
> I described it once as 'This head office was once a great back hole which sucked energy out of the units. Things vanished into it never to be seen again.' Whereas my idea of a head office is that it should be a tiny, tiny star in the sky, twinkling light down, completely out of the way.   (Interview)

Potentially, Lord Thurso faced major resistance to his integration plan. There was little alternative but to severely reduce the number of his central management team. While at the same time hinting at his future vision of restoring Champney's, Lord Thurso addressed the team as follows at a management meeting:

Please view my arrival not as something disastrous, but, actually, as an expansion of support by our shareholders.

The problem, in a nutshell, is that we are losing money. You are all intelligent people and therefore you will know that there will be a cost-cutting exercise. We have an expression in the fitness centre of 'no pain, no gain', but there will be pain.

We are, with the cost of head office, losing, as a company, approximately one million pounds in cash terms per year. It is my intention and target that, by the end of next year, we will be cash-breakeven. The direction I have decided to follow is to put Champney's, absolutely and without doubt, at the top of the tree.   (BBC 2)

He had decided to tell them collectively of his decision, so he delivered two clear and separate messages. The first message was that there was an compelling need to restructure and reduce the management resource. The second message was to specific individuals – that they were or were not, to be members of the future team.

Lord Thurso himself looked emotionally strained when he was asked how he felt about the restructuring process that had obviously proved very painful:

I would find it hard to sleep if I felt that anything I was doing was wrong in any way. I dislike doing it, but it a necessary operation that has to be done o the company. All that one can do is to do it as humanely and professionally as one can.

Most of them have been angry because, at the end of the day, we all like to think that we have a value in an organization and, effectively, when you are made redundant someone is saying that you don't have a value in the organization. When I say that it isn't to do with your performance, it is to entirely do with the financial structure of the company, it actually doesn't help them very much.   (BBC 2)

Acquisition integration is thus potentially highly emotionally and politically demanding, requiring a shift in skills set from the more analytical phases of acquisition strategy, due diligence and even of deal-making.

It is not hard to imagine what the atmosphere must have been like within the management team at Champney's as the reality sank in that it was the end of an era. It would be hard for those going, but those staying realized that they were expected to achieve a quantum shift in the level of effectiveness – if the business were to come back into profit.

It was then Lord Thurso's turn to address his operational staff. He appeared to be in a lighter mood as he informed his staff not merely about the severity of the situation, but also the fact that he was planning other job cuts:

> The last part of the strategy, and the bit that does concern all of you, is that New Court and the concept of a headquarters is going to be quite radically scaled down. There are 22 people sitting here and we have probably half the number of places actually available. You are intelligent and you will have worked this out. And therefore some people are going to have to be made redundant. . . . And I do recognize the pain that this will cause you. I am sorry that some of you will be going, but please understand that it is nothing to do with you and your capability. It is simply about how this business has been run over the past few years and the requirement to put it on a proper cash footing. (BBC 2)

Lord Thurso then tried to convey something of his vision, to try to inspire staff – thus positioning his integration strategy more positively:

> Finally, I would like to give you a little thought. All my life I have

been involved in giving first-class service to people and I believe it is a wonderful thing to do. Be always ready to say 'Yes' whenever a client or guest comes to see you and asks for something and you are tempted to say 'No'. Stop, think, and that will help us to create a level of service unheard of in this country. (BBC 2)

Besides dealing with internal stakeholders, Lord Thurso had to manage the expectations of Champney's members, whose business was needed to secure a successful future. These members had been disappointed in the past by the previous management who had, perhaps, set up expectations about improvements in standards that had not, or could not have, been delivered.

Lord Thurso was quick to realize that the 'Health-for-Life' time-sharing scheme needed to be halted. This scheme had been promoted to members as a way of getting more out of Champney's through building it into their life-styles. By acquiring a week's annual visit to Champney's, they could be confident in being a part of its exclusive heritage, while Champney's gained a secure regular revenue flow.

It had been intended that all of Champney's members would become time-share owners. Unfortunately the scheme was seen as very expensive and Champney's sales tactics (with a team of time-share salespeople) were perceived as being too pushy. Coming at a time of major recession in the UK, sales had been disappointing.

The new owner (and Lord Thurso) was apparently unaware of all the problems caused by the 'Health-for-Life' time-share. Apparently, when Champney's was purchased, many hundreds of time-share visits had been offered free to potential guests – and without a cut-off date. The contingent liability from these vouchers ran into several hundred thousand pounds (as a weekend visit – excluding treatments – then cost around £800 per couple). Lord Thurso told his team quite candidly:

> From what I have seen, the constant push-push-push on 'Health-for-Life' has given the wrong impression in the marketplace. I think maybe we should cut that right back.   (BBC 2)

An even bigger problem was that the physical facilities and amenities at Champney's did not provide a sustainable foundation for its future strategy:

> What a great architect friend of mine once described as the 'wow' factor. What we have got here is the 'er' factor. What we need is a 'wow' factors.   (BBC 2)

So, besides the organizational changes Lord Thurso instigated, he also set about developing an ambitious project to revitalize the physical fabric of Champney's. This included:

- A major upgrade in the entrance and facade to the central building – and to the driveway itself.

- Upgrade of the restaurant and other facilities – and an expansion in treatment rooms.

These renovations, Lord Thurso hoped, would provide a further benefit – signals to Champney's employees that the company was genuinely going to be set on the road to a prosperous future. But the final cost for these improvements was £6.75 million.

The integration plan

To achieve his integration plans, Lord Thurso needed to build the confidence of his investors, who might well have thought that a turnaround was possible without major investment of this order. Lord Thurso realized that, to provide the basis for this confidence, he would need to achieve a number of things in Phase 1 of integration:

- The restructuring of management had to be implemented successfully.

- Better financial planning and control needed to be stabilized – with the help of the new Finance Director, who Lord Thurso had brought in.

- His restructuring would need to have delivered the required cost savings.

- Although a gap still remained (to break even) with these cost savings, this gap would need to be closed by expanding revenues.

- To achieve this, the quality of service and standards generally at Champney's had to improve considerably – to the point where members felt a real difference and new members were brought in. To this end Lord Thurso brought in a new and very tough General Manager.

Although cost savings of half a million pounds per annum were achieved relatively quickly, it proved much slower to improve sales by improving customer confidence. However, within one year Champney's had managed to break even. So, Lord Thurso was able to then put into effect his plan to obtain enough investment to reposition Champney's as an outstanding health resort.

His overseas investor was able to give Lord Thurso the vote of confidence he needed in order to move on to implementing Phase 2 of the integration – a major upgrading programme. So, at last, all the planks of Lord Thurso's integration strategy were in place.

Managing the integration – the dynamics

It is also necessary to look at how implementation difficulty changes over time. Figure 9.2 gives an approximate view of this 'difficulty over time' curve. Initially, Lord Thurso's turnaround faced severe difficulties, but, once the new structure was in place, and once Lord Thurso's new vision for the organization had been unveiled, this difficulty would be mitigated.

However, as time progressed, this difficulty might well have increased as the organization found a new stability and sought to resist further changes. In turn, this difficulty might then begin to reduce once Lord

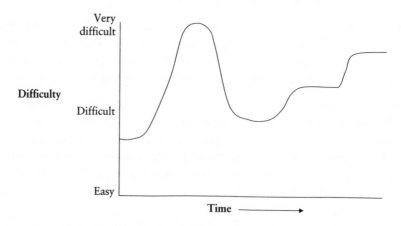

Figure 9.2 Integration difficulty–time curve for Champney's.

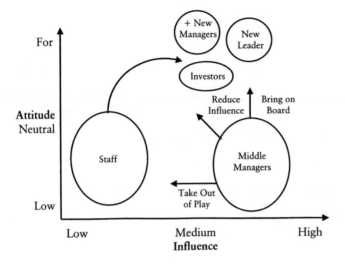

Figure 9.3 Champney's stakeholder analysis.

Thurso's programmes to improve customer service and to shift attitudes began to bite.

Next, Figure 9.3 plots the approximate positions of some of the key stakeholders who had an influence on his integration plan. This diagram highlights that before Lord Thurso unveiled his integration plan, the balance of influence in the organizations was against him. Equally, by introducing new stakeholders, exiting some old ones and by appealing directly to the staff, the balance of influence was reversed – in Lord Thurso's favour.

Obviously, this picture is drawn at a relatively high level. If we were to go down to a deeper level (that of the agendas of individual stakeholders) we would clearly find difference in the attitudes of individuals within these groupings.

The reason why stakeholder analysis is so important during acquisition integration is that unless key stakeholders are on board, shareholder value will be destroyed in an myriad of ways. These include:

- Disruption through key staff leaving.

- Costs of recruitment and of new staff.

- Knock-on effects of staff levels, through lost customers.

- Difficulty of obtaining new orders due to negative stories reaching customers about decline in organizational competence following staff losses.

- Staff distraction causing them to become less productive or attentive to quality and achievement of deadlines.

- No new really thrusting development of products, services or processes during the period of uncertainty.

By undertaking a robust stakeholder analysis it is much easier to manage the communication strategy, to focus restructuring, and to re-motivate staff at all levels.

Influencing stakeholders, equally, demands considerable leadership skills and also a clear vision for the integration on the part of the integrating manager. Lord Thurso elaborates:

> You need a lot of managers in a business who don't necessarily have to be a leader themselves. But you damn well need one leader.
>
> (Interview)

- The agendas of stakeholders are not fixed, but will change over time as new issues arise and perceptions change within the organization.

- At any point in time, agendas may be fluid and ambiguous, particularly at the start of the turnaround. Key stakeholders, particularly middle managers, may not have any clear attitude at all. Although they may have some core agendas (such as 'I want to hang on to my job'), these might be very limited. Even here, core agendas might be conditional on Champney's being seen as a congenial atmosphere to work in, given its new leadership. Never assume, therefore, that attitudes and underlying agendas of stakeholders are always given.

- Individuals within one group will influence the agendas of others within the group. Via the informal network, opinion leaders will signal their approval or disapproval of particular actions.

- You may need to break down the change into a number of subgroups – as stakeholder positions will vary according to what is being implemented.

The integration required the various changes Lord Thurso making being bedded down in the organization. This required strong management of operational improvement during 1997–1999 – and of ongoing culture change. This can be a long haul in the process, as Lord Thurso reflects:

> But the key figure at the top should have a kind of evangelical fanaticism about what the strategy is. Unless you have this, you are not going to manage to convince people. For example, last year I called our plans 'going from good to great'. And we didn't go from good to great we got better. So I said 'This is good to great part II', We could be back here next year doing part III or even part IV, but one day we will get there and I ain't leaving here until we do.

Case postscript

Champney's has now successfully:

- Been refurbished, and had attracted back many of its traditional clientele.

- Expanded its business significantly – at the core Tring site.

- Refurbished its satellite centre at Piccadilly, London, opened a further small facility in central London and another in Brussels.

- Was looking into further plans to develop its network and distribution channels.

- And was profitable, but still seeking to increase its return on capital.

- Was thus on a new stage of strategy development (Phase 4 of its integration strategy).

- Now being managed by its new Chief Executive, Lord Thurso having moved into full-time politics.

Summary

Post-acquisition integration is the key to capturing a positive value for V3. Integration difficulties may be due to poorly thought-through integration strategies, or to organizational constraints, or to poor project management.

Generally speaking, the more successful integrative strategies appear to be where there is great clarity, early implementation, decisive follow-through, close monitoring and continuous learning. It also

Smart lessons from Champney's

In summary, here are the key pointers to the acquisition champion for managing acquisitions.

- An integration strategy must be thought out in detail before completion, and not afterwards.
- Central to this strategy is the choice of the integration manager – here put in place only after completion.
- Clear targets need to be set in terms of (a) cash generation, (b) profits and (c) shareholder value generation – medium and longer term.
- Operations due diligence needs to get a grip on how the company is competing at a micro-level: to flush out issues like the free 'Health-for-Life' vouchers – rather than simply being a set of preconceived factual checklists. Also, wherever possible, try to simulate being a customer of the organization you are trying to acquire (just as Lord Thurso sampled the treatments).
- Be more creative and radical in thinking about options for integration – these are far more extensive in the case study than perhaps those considered by Champney's.
- Scope the iceberg of investment required to deliver fully successful integration; and be realistic about which returns you will then get.
- Be radical and stretching in thinking through organizational options – go for 'what you really-really want', and not just work from what you inherit.
- Break the integration process up into phases (or stages) – and project manage it against clear milestones.
- Stakeholder management is absolutely central to the integration process. Accordingly, ample time should be devoted to analysing the current and potentially future positions of stakeholders – and their driving agendas.
- Leadership is crucial in a situation where stakeholders are likely to actively resist integration efforts. This leadership requires a degree of evangelical enthusiasm, a very explicit statement about the strategic vision and great practical tenacity in implementing that vision.
- Achieving headway depends not merely on forward progress, but on building a sufficient 'stakeholder platform' that can be used to achieve leverage from during restructuring. This involved (at Champney's) key appointments of a new Finance Director and a General Manager – and winning over Champney's front-line staff.
- The difficulty over time of the integration needs to be thought through.

Acquisition integration

- For an acquisition you are thinking of making:
- What would the key stages of integration (phases 1–4) look like?
- What would you need to accomplish in each stage?
- How would you seek to accomplish this (what key projects would be needed)?

highlighted the fact that it was generally easier to realize 'sweat value' than any other terms of value. At BMW and Rover we saw the need to anticipate scenarios of the future, and to make integration interventions sooner and more decisively. This highlighted the 'investment iceberg' of acquisitions, which often become visible only through integration. At Champney's we revealed the effort that was needed to deliver value through integration and through further investment.

Case Postscript

In August 2002 Champney's was sold (for an undisclosed sum) to Purdew Health Group, as part of the latter's growth strategy. Purdew runs the less up-market Henlow Grange, Springs, Fastmere and Inglewood health and fitness centres. It will be interesting to see what its future integration strategies are for Champney's, and how it will be successful in increasing, rather than destroying, its shareholder value.

10

Conclusion

The role of acquisitions – a review

Acquisitions have in the past principally destroyed, rather than created, shareholder value. But for those that failed, it is relatively straightforward to identify the reason – given the concepts and techniques in this book – and how this might have been avoided.

The most successful acquisitions tend to be ones where:

- There is a close degree of relatedness – especially of competencies.

- You are not acquiring in markets which are vulnerable to intensified competitive pressures.

- You are getting a company which is not in a fundamentally weak competitive position.

- Either very strong management skills are already in place, or can be readily brought in during integration.

- You have deployed a sufficient range of skills, especially:

- strategic

- commercial

- operational

- change management

- project management

- financial

- legal and taxation

- HR and pensions etc.

[See Allen and Hodgkinson (1986) for more on due diligence in the latter areas.]

Diagnosis of your own skills and weakenesses

To become an effective acquisition champion requires in-depth capability in all of the skills mentioned in the last section. For some skills, like legal and taxation, you will probably require either internal or external advisers or experts. But other skills areas are perhaps far more crucial to have – otherwise you will be unable to ask the right questions, at the right time, throughout the process.

To test out your skills gaps, use the following to profile your biggest areas of strength and weaknesses. Notice just how broad and stretching the prerequisite range of skills is for acquisitions.

Skill area	Weak 1	Slightly weaker 2	Average 3	Strong 4	Very strong 5
Strategic analysis					
Strategic options/decisions					
Marketing skills					
Market awareness (specific to the acquisition)					
Operational diagnosis					
Organizational structuring					

Judging management strengths
and weaknesses

Change management

Financial analysis

Financial planning

Negotiating

Legal knowledge

Taxation knowledge

Pensions knowledge

Project management

Integration processes

Preparing an acquisition business
case

Managing external advisers

Experience of systems integration

Leadership of acquisition teams
(or working in them)

Now add up your score; which will be out of 100.

80–100:   You are Superman!

60–80:   Well done – a case of continuous management

40–80:   Work on your major gaps.

20–40:   Don't get disheartened – get a junior team role.

A candid, analytical evaluation of acquisition experiences is often difficult in firms. Few decisions rival acquisitions in their propensity to label a manager's career. As a result, the retroactive interpretation of acquisition events serves the political ends of protecting some managers' careers or attaching a stigma to others.

P.C. Haspeslagh and D.B. Jemison, *Managing Acquisitions*

Acquisitions and your career

Acquisition can be of great benefit to your career in a number of areas:

- By being involved in the acquisition appraisal you will develop your strategic and general management skills – at an accelerated pace.

- By being an acquisition champion you might be able to cut your teeth on its integration, playing a role in its senior management.

- Integration management will enable you to much improve and sharpen your implementation, project management and change management skills.

- Acquisition experience can lead to a senior specialist role in for example, strategic planning or in business development.

- It is ideal experience prior to doing an MBA (or indeed for practising MBA skills – for the newly qualified MBA).

- It will also look absolutely great on your CV.

- Managing an acquisition successfully will be a major boost to your confidence generally.

So I now conclude by wishing you a prosperous, stimulating and disaster free future role as

Acquisition Champion

Bibliography

Allen, M. and Hodgkinson (1986) *Buying a Business*. Graham and Trotman, London.

Ansoff, H. I. (1965) *Corporate Strategy*. McGraw-Hill, New York.

Copeland, T., Koller, T. and Murrin, J. (1990) *Valuation: Measuring and Managing the Value of Companies*. John Wiley, New York.

Faulkner, D. (1995) *International Strategic Alliances*. McGraw-Hill, Maidenhead.

Faulkner, D. and Bowman, C. (1995) *The Essence of Competitive Strategy*. Prentice Hall, Englewood Cliffs, NJ.

Gould, M., Campbell, A. and Alexander, M. (1994) *Corporate-level Strategy*. John Wiley, New York.

Grundy, A. N. (1995) *Breakthrough Strategies for Growth*. FT Pitman, London.

Grundy, A. N. (1998) *Exploring Strategic Financial Management*. Prentice Hall, London.

Hammer, M. and Champy, J. (1993) *Re-engineering the Corporation*. Nicolas Brealey, London.

Haspeslagh, P. C. and Jemison, D. B. (1991) *Managing Acquisitions – Creating Value Through Corporate Renewal*. The Free Press/Macmillan, New York.

Jemison, J. B. and Sitkin, S. B. (1986) Acquisitions – the process can be a problem. *Harvard Business Review*, March–April, 107–116.

Koch, R. (1995) *The Financial Times Guide to Strategy*. Financial Times, London.

McTaggart, J. M., Kontes, P. W. and Mankins, M. C. (1994) *The Value Imperative*. The Free Press/Macmillan, New York.

Mills, R. W. (1994) *Strategic Value Analysis*. Mars Business Associates, Lechlade.

Mintzberg, H. (1994) *The Rise and Fall of Strategic Planning*. Prentice Hall, Hemel Hempstead.

Ohmae, K. (1982) 'The Mind of the Strategist', New York, McGraw-Hill.

Porter, E. M. (1980) *Competitive Strategy*. The Free Press/Macmillan, New York

Porter, E. M. (1987) From competitive advantage to corporate strategy. *Harvard Business Review*, May–June, 43–59.

Rappaport, A. (1986) *Creating Shareholder Value*. The Free Press/Macmillan, New York.

Sirower, M. L. (1997) *The Synergy Trap*. The Free Press, New York.

Sparks, J. D. (1999) Mastering strategy. *Financial Times Series*, Autumn.

Stewart, G. Bennet, III (1991) *The Quest for Value – The EVA Management Guide*. HarperBusiness, New York.

Index

products/services
  due diligence 114
  evaluation 110–14
  market analysis 109
  markets/marketing 103
  organizations/people 104
  technology 104

Rappaport, A. 145
risk *see* uncertainty/risk
Rover Group 32, 92, 105, 113, 127
  acquisition characteristics 17–18
  assumptions concerning 153–5
  deal process 178–83
  disposal to Phoenix 193–5
  organization/people 119
  performance drivers 208–10
  strategic position (1994) 65–70
  technology dependency on alliance
      118
  value/cost drivers 129–30

search process 21–2, 25, 78–9
  approaching a target 81–2
  co-ordination 76–8
  deal-making considerations 82–3
  decentralization 77
  financial brokers 80–1
  market, competitive/competitor
      analysis 79–80
  summary 83–4
shareholder value
  segmenting the value 21–2
  three 'V's 14–15
  types of acquisition 16–20
  understanding 13–14
Sirower, M.L. 22, 128, 146, 154, 188

Sitkin, S.B. 13
Sparkes, Jack D. 28
stakeholder
  acceptability 55, 96–8
  analysis 204–7
strategic attractiveness 86–9
strategy 3, 21, 24–5
  acquisition options 49–52
    financial attractiveness 53–4
    implementation difficulty 54–5
    stakeholder acceptability 55
    strategic attractiveness 52–3
  championing 39–43
  competitive advantage 41
  criteria
    acquisition don'ts 57
    acquisition do's 56
    determining 57–8
  cunning plan 40–2
  external evaluation 59–62
    case study 62–71
  gap analysis 45–8
  head-start 11
  internal evaluation 71–2
  model 20
  objectives/goals 43
    competitive 44
    customer 44
    defined 44
    financial 44–5
    market positioning 44
  open/emergent 40
  process considerations 72–4
  summary 74
  target market/environment 42
SWOT analysis 43